ONE SIMPLE
EQUATION

ONE SIMPLE EQUATION

$$F=TL^3$$

David N. Heizer

ELM HILL

A Division of
HarperCollins Christian Publishing

www.elmhillbooks.com

One Simple Equation

$F=TL^3$

Published in Nashville, Tennessee, by Elm Hill, an imprint of Thomas Nelson. Elm Hill and Thomas Nelson are registered trademarks of HarperCollins Christian Publishing, Inc.

Elm Hill titles may be purchased in bulk for educational, business, fund-raising, or sales promotional use. For information, please e-mail SpecialMarkets@ ThomasNelson.com.

Library of Congress Cataloging-in-Publication Data

Library of Congress Control Number: 2019918914

ISBN 978-1-400329953 (Paperback)
ISBN 978-1-400329960 (Hardbound)
ISBN 978-1-400329977 (eBook)

ACKNOWLEDGEMENTS

I would like to thank the following for their inspiration and guidance. Thank you God our Father for your steadfast love and grace. Jesus for the sacrifice you endured for our salvation. Mom, Dad and Scott for a warm loving family full of support and guidance. Shauna Pierce for being by my side through the best and the worst, for being a wonderful stepmom, my love and friend. Newton and Zoe, I love you and am very proud of you both. Frank And Trish Angilella for accepting my family as your own. Matt and Erin Blair for your passion and love for Christ and planting Limitless Church. Jonathan Her, Scott Bishop, Jenny Figueroa, Melanie De Leon, Taylor Nay, George Wood and Erin Blair for sharing your courageous testimonies and love of Christ. Cory, Jen, Xander, Ayden, and Eli Evans for simply being family. Jim Mitchell, Steve Beyer and Steve Schmalhorst for being warriors in prayer. Jacob and Thad Smith for your enlightening theological discussions. Bill Martin for teaching me more about the Bible and scripture than I could have learned on my own. Angel Mitchell and Laura Martin for opening your homes giving our small group two warm and comfortable places to find community and friendship. Jeremy Hager for being the first believer in this book. Matt and Brianna Timmons, Colin McGinn and Jacob Barrineau for pouring into my children and being great role models. David Hitchcock for your thoughtful conversations and friendship. Charlotte Furey for you warm smiles. Matt and Molly Trapuzzano,

Rafael Abreu and Nelvy Ruiz for being good friends. Brandon and Breanna Blocker for your partnership and belief in this book. Deno Kazanis, Ph.D. for your insights into science and spirituality. Mount Saint Joseph High School for planting a seed of faith in the darkest corner of my heart that would eventually grow and bear fruit. To the rest of my family at Limitless Church and Humana for years of love and friendship. Thank you all.

TABLE OF CONTENTS

An Unlikely Christian

An unlikely Christian. Growing up, if you were to ask any of my childhood friends if I would ever find myself following Christ, they would probably say, "That would be a cold day in hell." I grew up an atheist. My mother was raised Catholic but had a bad taste for the Catholic Church. My father was raised in a house religiously sterile as far as I know and was a self-proclaimed atheist for as long as I can remember. So, when it came to raising my brother and me, there was no mention of God, church, or religion in our home. A few neighbors attended church, but it just wasn't a focus in our community. As I grew older, several of my friends did attend church on Sunday morning, and my brother and I patiently waited for them to return so we could get all the neighborhood kids out playing together.

Despite the lack of church and God in our household as a child, my parents were very loving parents to me and my brother. We didn't know cold, sterile parents; we knew warm, loving parents who attended all our school functions and sporting events. Mom spent years chauffeuring my brother and me to swimming practices twice a day. My parents were very supportive. We were a close family with close ties to our extended family members. I had a very normal middle-class upbringing. Holidays were spent with family, aunts, uncles, and cousins alike. We all got along very well and I was left with fond memories of my childhood. We were all very happy to the best of my recollection.

My brother and I, only being eleven months apart, had the same friends growing up. Out of all the neighborhood houses, ours was where all our friends congregated. My mom was always cooking for our friends. Everyone was always welcome for dinner. Even as adults, our friends always invited our parents to their weddings and birthday parties for their kids. Our friends seemed to enjoy and love my parents as much as my brother and I did. As business owners, my parents were loved by their employees and were very generous and kind employers. The absence of God and church didn't seem to impede our family life very much at all from my point of view at the time. It is so clear to me now, though, that God was there in our home. He was there pouring His love into all four of us each and every day. We just had not looked up to see it or even accept it.

My maternal grandfather passed away when I was in eighth grade from cancer. He was very excited prior to his death about my parents' decision to send me to a Catholic high school. He had converted to Catholicism when he married my grandmother and he was a deeply spiritual man. So, off to Catholic school I went with absolutely no under-standing of Christianity. I took a religion class each of the four years I attended high school, but due to a lack of interest and understanding, I treated it like any other history class. Just a series of events that happened long ago. That is what it seemed like to me—just another history class. I missed the whole idea of the Gospel. That is not a slight on the high school I attended; it was a wonderful school and I received a great educa-tion. It afforded me opportunities I might not have had from the public school system in that area back in the early 1980s. I was the problem. I chose to ignore the good news being shared with me.

As a matter of fact, I believe that Mount Saint Joseph High School actually planted the seeds my faith would grow from thirty years later.

After high school, I attended college on a swimming scholarship. College was the period of my life that marked a real change in me. This change was not a positive one. It was a dark time for me. I was in the process of embarking on my life's journey into the world—separated from the warm comforts of childhood, loving parents, and a sense that all was going to be okay because my parents were taking care of me. Now, I was on my own. I had to make decisions that would have a profound impact on my future. I was terrified. Because there was an absence of God in my life anchoring me to a correct path, I turned to alcohol and partying to raise my spirits; a lifestyle that took me down a path of uncertainty, depression, poor choices, and unhappiness.

I felt very lost in those years. College was just one long party punctuated with having to go to swim practice, classes, and the need to get a degree. I dropped off the swim team after my junior year to join a fraternity. I gave up seventeen years of training as a swimmer to party harder than I ever had before. I graduated in the spring of 1990 which I thought of as a miracle. I had somehow deciphered the riddle of test taking in college and became a master test taker despite the wild partying and drinking I was doing back then. Thirty years later, I truly believe it was the loving hand of God carrying me through a difficult time. I never could have graduated from college without God's help. I just hadn't made the choice to see it yet. It will actually be many more years before I finally do make that choice.

After college, I started to question my purpose in this world so I turned to books of science, biology, physics, paleontology, and cosmology. As I read about the wonders of string theory, black holes, the Big Bang, biological evolution, and the fossil record, I started to formulate thoughts and ideas on my own existence. How the human race and ultimately how I got here. It was all rooted in the science I was reading. I never once had the inkling to check into theology. I believed that was the stuff of fantasy and mystics.

I would spend the next twenty years chasing selfish, materialistic dreams; searching for fulfillment in all the wrong places. That was until my change of heart and a profound change in my way of thinking. My change of heart began in early 2012 while going through a devastating divorce and being diagnosed with cancer all at the same time. That change of heart would take several years, God's love, a powerful mathematical equation, a loving partner, and two pastors with a tremendous passion for Jesus.

I was someone who didn't believe in God, now I do. I was someone who never had time for attending church regularly, now I do. I was someone who didn't have time to serve at church or serve others, now I do. I was someone who didn't have time to participate in small groups outside of Sunday services, now I do. As you will read in the chapters of this book, it was God's *love* as the anchor, the constant term in the most powerful equation I have ever encountered that became the driving force behind this unlikely Christian.

CHAPTER 1

JUST LOVE

"For God so loved the world that he gave his one and only Son, that whoever believes in him shall not perish but have eternal Life."

(JOHN 3:16 NIV)

Just love. Two simple yet dynamic words that take on so much meaning. These two words can be a command—God's desire for us—to "just" love God and "just" love our neighbor as ourselves. These two words can be a question. Just love? Is that all we need to do? We just need to love God and our neighbor as ourselves? Just love can imply that love is just in a legalistic sense. Is God's love just? No matter the context we apply to these two words, "just love," it is imperative that one sees the importance of the command, that one answers the question with an affirmative, and that one understands that God's love is just. God's love for each one of us is the anchor of our faith. It is the one constant in the universe that is steadfast and never failing. God's love is where we are to place all our trust.

One simple equation changed everything for me. Jesus is so simple yet we as humans tend to complicate him. We believe he is far more complicated than he really is. Like Jesus, the equation I am going to introduce you to is simple as well, even if it looks complicated to you the reader. Together, we will learn how to use this one simple equation to reaffirm our faith, to open a simple dialog with others using it as a simple tool for discipling, to unlock the very nature of *truth, free will, good and evil*, and *the meaning of life*.

"Love the Lord your God with all your heart and with all your soul and with all your mind."

(MATTHEW 22:37 NIV)

Several years ago, God placed an equation expressing faith on my heart. This is an equation that expresses Christian faith specifically. $F = TL^3$. **Faith** equals our **trust** times **God's love** cubed or to the power of three. The three terms in this equation are not random terms plucked from thin air, they were extrapolated carefully from the Bible—the written Word of God. We will read in the chapters ahead just how important these three simple yet profound terms are and how this equation can impact our lives on a daily basis.

God's love is the cornerstone of this book and the equation $F = TL^3$. God has put this on my heart to be a simple illustration of our *faith*. The reader can easily visualize the primary components of faith when looking at the equation. Christians can pray over the equation in times of hardship. It is often during those difficult times when we pull away from God. When we struggle with our finances, our relationships, our jobs, etc., we typically turn away from God and his promise that was given to us out of his love for us. We think that we have to bear the heavy load, make decisions, work harder and harder to get through whatever the struggle is. We live in a broken world and are surrounded by broken people. As a result of this brokenness, we will all experience difficulties throughout our lives. Placing our trust in God and believing in his promises will get us through those tough times. Having the faith that "God has this" is the answer. It isn't always easy, after all, we are human. We do sin and we make mistakes. Praying over God's love for us does make a difference and this equation can help to visualize clearly what to pray over.

"Father, please give me the strength and wisdom to place all my trust in your love; so through your love, I can have peace and joy in the knowledge that you have this, Father; that through your love, I will get past all that causes me worry, anxiety, and fear. Thank you for your steadfast love, Father."

Christians can meditate and pray on this equation in times of good fortune as well. This is when we often forget about God. We become boastful and start to believe the product of our success is of our own means. This is a dangerous mindset. By meditating and praying on the equation $F = TL^3$, we can put our focus back on God's love for us and the truth that it was God who blessed us in these moments of good fortune. We can then thank God for the provision and keep ourselves in a right relationship with God. When life seems to be going so well, knowing that God's love for you has been the giving force behind the blessings you receive here in this world will ensure that you don't lose sight of who the giver is. God is the giver.

The equation $F = TL^3$ is also an easy way to express our faith to those around us. We can become better disciples by having a blueprint for a conversation. This equation can be a simple plug and play blueprint for a discipling conversation. We can illustrate this by replacing God's love with any idolatrous term. If someone tries to replace God's love with any other term, the equation falls apart. You can't replace God's love with money, power, wealth, beauty, sex, drugs, or any other idolatrous term without breaking down the value of faith. Complete trust in anything but God's love establishes a disastrous foundation for a person's faith. In the following chapters, I will take the reader through specific exercises to better illustrate this idea.

Why express our Christian faith as a mathematical equation $F = TL^3$? First, mathematics is a universal language. The language of mathematics is the one language every human being on the planet can speak. Mathematical concepts are understood by all people regardless of ethnicity, nationality, language, or culture. No matter where on earth a person is from, the idea of 1+1=2 is generally understood. Even a person who lives deep in a jungle with little to no education knows that, if they pick up one coconut from the jungle floor then pick up another coconut, they now have two coconuts regardless of the word they use for the number two. The words sound different—"two" in English, "*dos*" in Spanish, "*deux*" in French, "*zwei*" in German, and "*mbili*" in Swahili—even so, the concept of "two" remains the same. More complex mathematical disciplines such as geometry, algebra, calculus, trigonometry, or quantum mechanics are understood the same way by mathematicians and scientists from around the world. Algebra in the United States is the same as algebra in Spain, Portugal, India, or any other country. Mathematics is defined as the abstract science of number, quantity, and space (*Oxford Living Dictionary*).

Our brains perform mathematical calculations all the time, most of which we are not even conscious of. For example, if you have ever thrown a ball to your child, your child's brain has to calculate the trajectory of the ball and the speed of the ball to determine where in three dimensional space to place his or her hand to intercept the ball and catch it. Our brains perform mathematical calculations to walk across a crowded room or drive a car on a busy road. Mathematics is a part of our everyday life. Whether we are aware of it or not, we all calculate mathematically the world around us every day of our lives.

The idea that mathematical concepts are universally understood regardless of nationality, culture, or language makes it very easy to have a real discussion about our faith when we express it mathematically. $F = TL^3$ is concise and easy to understand. As I will discuss shortly, the more trust we place in God's love, the stronger our faith becomes. It all hinges on God's love for us.

Second, mathematics is not just a universal language among humans, it is the language of God himself. Everything that is seen, detected, or measured in the visible universe can be expressed mathematically. Scientists and mathematicians can express light being emitted from the sun and distant stars, the molecular structure of compounds, how the planets, stars, and galaxies swirl through the cosmos, and the human genome mathematically. Even things we experience in our day-to-day lives can be expressed mathematically, such as traffic patterns on our roadways to the computer programs we use every day. If you are reading these words on a computer, tablet, or smartphone, the app used to allow you to read this book electronically was designed using mathematical concepts. So, why shouldn't we be able to express our faith mathematically?

As Christians, we believe that God created the universe and everything in it. The Book of Genesis, the first book of the Bible, tells us that God spoke everything into existence. This implies that God used a language to speak the universe into existence; I believe He used the language of mathematics. Each act of creation from Genesis 1:1 through Genesis 1:31 begins with "And God said." "And God said, 'Let there be light'" (Genesis 1:3 NIV). "And God said, 'Let there be a vault between the waters to separate water from water'" (Genesis 1:6 NIV). "And God said, 'Let the water under the sky be gathered to one place'" (Genesis 1:9 NIV). "Then God said, 'Let the land produce vegetation'" (Genesis 1:11 NIV). "And God said, 'Let there be lights in the vault of the sky'" (Genesis 1:14 NIV). "And God said, 'Let the water teem with living creatures, and let birds fly above the earth across the vault of the sky'" (Genesis 1:20 NIV). "And God said, 'Let the land bring forth living creatures according to their kinds'" (Genesis 1:24 ESV). "Then God said, 'Let us make mankind in **our** image, in **our** likeness…'" (Genesis 1:26 NIV, emphasis mine). God spoke the universe into existence using a language, the language of mathematics, which in its basic form can be understood by all people. Everywhere we look in the visible universe, we see God's creation, we see God's Word. God spoke the very fabric of the universe into existence by weaving it together with threads spun from the wool of mathematics.

The Bible uses numbers and calculations extensively. Numbers are very important and have deep meaning throughout many books of the

Bible. My favorite prophetic calculation can be found in the Book of Daniel 9:24–27. Five hundred thirty-eight years before Jesus was born, Daniel prophesied or calculated to the day when Jesus, the Messiah, would enter the world and die on the cross. Daniel's calculation begins on the date March 5, 444 BC, and ends on the date March 30, 33 AD. The total number of days between these two dates is 173,880 days. In the dynamic prophecy of the seventy weeks, Daniel calculated there would be sixty-nine intervals of seven years from the date of the decree to rebuild Jerusalem in 444 BC and the death by execution for the sins of others of the Messiah in 33 AD. Knowing that the calendar in that historical time period only had 360 days per year, we can count the number of days between the date of the decree on March 5th, 444 BC and the date of Jesus' death on March 30th, 33 AD. That number is a mind-blowing 173,880 days exactly: $69 \times 7 \times 360 = 173{,}880$. There is a lot more to this prophecy and I have simplified it for the purposes of this book. I would urge you to read the Book of Daniel for a full understanding of the dates and calculations illustrated in this prophecy. I truly love how God uses numbers and calculations throughout the Bible.

Third, as I mentioned above, $F = TL^3$ is a simple expression that we can easily meditate and pray on when contemplating our faith. During difficult times when our faith is being tested, we can meditate and pray on just how much trust we are placing in God's love for us. This is an exercise that can help the reader push through those difficult seasons that seem to distance us from God. By focusing on our trust in God's love, we can be reminded that God is always with us, pursuing us. He will not leave us. Understanding this is the first step to regaining our closeness with God and to knowing that we will get through whatever the struggle, whether it is money, kids, relationships, work, etc. Worry and anxiety are a result of our losing trust in or not even knowing that God "has this." We can know that God does "have this" by knowing just how much he loves us. By reapplying lost trust in God's love, worry, anxiety, and fear can melt away. God will provide exactly what we need when we need it. He always does. Granted it is not always when we think we need it or even want it. The older I get, the more I can reflect on God's perfect timing for my life. We can apply this equation to our prayer time with God and pray: *"Father, give me the wisdom to place ALL my trust in your love because you LOVED me so much you were willing to die for me so I may live. Thank you, Father, for your unfailing love."* Through prayers like this, we can know that our faith is being strengthened and our relationship with God is being renewed daily.

Fourth, the equation $F = TL^3$ can be used as a tool to help us disciple. We are all called to be disciples. **"Therefore go and make disciples of all nations, baptizing them in the name of the Father and of the Son and of the Holy Spirit" (Matthew 28:19 NIV).** As Christians, we tend to neglect that command because we don't know how to start the conversation, or we don't want to offend anyone, or we are just fearful of what we don't know. Some people think they need a PhD in theology to refute all the objections they think the secular population is going to throw at them. The equation $F = TL^3$ can be a conversation starter. Christians can explain that God's constant, steadfast love is where they place all their trust. If any nonbeliever says they prefer to put their trust in worldly things like money, power, or even one's self, the reader can simply show how substituting the triune love of God with anything else at all, the equation falls apart as the product, faith, becomes shaky and very unstable. The finite objects of the material world are not foundational and therefore not suitable or constant terms on which to build our faith. Furthermore, faith in worldly things leads to worry, anxiety, and uncertainty. I will discuss in detail how this substitution for God's love fails on every occasion in subsequent chapters of this book.

CHAPTER 2

AN INSPIRATION

The equation $F = TL^3$ was inspired by Einstein's theory of relativity as expressed by the equation $E = mc^2$. Energy is equal to mass ("m" the variable) times the speed of light ("c" the constant 186,000 miles per second) squared. The beauty and simplicity of Einstein's equation is breathtaking. The theory has stood up for over a century since it was introduced in 1905 expressing what we observe in the cosmos.

The idea of a faith equation came to me several years ago as I was contemplating the equation $E = mc^2$ and speed of light travel. I was imagining how I could travel at the speed of light. According to Einstein's theory, I would have to become massless to travel at the speed of light, which is why only massless particles like photons travel at the speed they do. Very simply stated, mass is a measure of how much matter or material is in an object and is measured in grams or kilograms. When matter is exposed to gravity, it has weight. Since the moon has a different gravity, then Earth objects with the same mass weigh differently on the moon than they would on Earth, but their mass would remain the same. If an object is massless, the object would be weightless regardless of how much or how little gravity it was exposed to.

That day, while contemplating Einstein's theory, I wondered how I could accomplish the feat of becoming massless and came to the conclusion—perhaps my soul is massless and in death, I could travel at the speed of light, allowing me to experience aspects of the theory like time stopping completely from the perspective of the traveler. I could then travel billions of miles through space in an instant from my perspective. Time slows down from the perspective of the traveler as the speed of light is approached and stops completely at 186,000 miles per second. I then thought perhaps, we will all have the ability to travel this way in heaven. Could my heavenly experience be realized by zipping around the great expanse of God's creation at the speed of light, allowing millions even billions of years to pass instantly? After all, I will be in heaven for eternity, trillions and trillions of years and beyond. I thought, *That would be really cool.* This led me to start thinking about heaven, God, and my faith. I began to wonder if my faith could be expressed in a similar way; in the form of an equation. If I could express my faith in a mathematical equation, I could then meditate on my faith much like when I was meditating on becoming massless and traveling at the speed of light. This seemed to be a very exciting proposition. Perhaps I could also use such an equation to help others find their way to Jesus Christ.

So, I set out to attempt to develop such an equation. I identified the term I wanted to solve for—"faith"; my faith in God and Jesus as my savior in particular, even though I had not yet completely committed my life to Jesus at the time. But I was on a collision course with the life-changing realization that I would have to make that commitment to Christ Jesus before long. It would still be another two years before I was baptized.

Faith is the foundation, the cornerstone on which we all establish our principles by which to live. So, faith, being such an important aspect of our humanity, seemed like the perfect term to solve for. After deciding to solve for the term "faith," I needed to figure out just how to do that. I thought about the question, "What is my faith?" My faith is what I believed to be true even if I couldn't prove it empirically. It is what I trust as being truth. I came to the conclusion that trust was an appropriate term to use as a variable in the equation as our trust in anything will vary from day to day. My trust in anything varies as a result of my ever-changing circumstances from one day to the next. Trust is also a factor in faith as faith can be defined as trusting in something that cannot necessarily be proven. *Now, I just need the constant term in the equation,* I thought to myself. This was easy as nothing is more constant and steadfast as God's love for us. So love, God's love, became the constant term for the equation. I thought it still needed more, though. Perhaps, the full love of God or the triune love of God. The love of the Father, the Son, and the Holy Spirit. *Yes!* I thought. Love cubed is what I was looking for. God's love could be raised to the power of three to represent the trinity.

I was inspired by Einstein's equation $E = mc^2$ as I developed $F = TL^3$ and what I refer to as a "beautiful expression of faith." Beautiful for its simplicity. It also fits into the idea of Occam's razor quite well. Occam's razor states, *"Given several possible explanations for something, the simplest one is probably correct."* I have expanded somewhat on this idea to give you the following: *"Everything in the visible universe can be expressed mathematically. Everything else is expressed experientially. The most beautiful and accurate expressions are those expressed with the greatest degree of simplicity."* The path to everlasting life with God is a very simple path. It may not be easy but it is simple. We simply have to accept that Jesus is our savior. That he died on the cross as the final sacrifice, freeing us from our debt of sin and that he rose from the dead three days later as proof of everlasting life. The more trust we place in God's love, the easier it is to accept Jesus as our savior. As we place our full trust in God's love for us, we can understand why God sent Jesus in the first place and see it as truth. "F" (faith) equals "T" (trust—the variable) times "L" (God's love; the constant—*infinite and limitless*) cubed. In this equation, the cubed refers to the Trinity—the Father, Son, and Holy Spirit or the triune love of God.

Let's look at the equation a little closer.

"And without faith it is impossible to please God, because any-one who comes to him must believe that he exists and that he rewards those who earnestly seek after him"

(Hebrews 11:6 NIV)

"F" equals trust times God's love cubed. "F" represents the term for "faith" which is what we will be solving for since faith is the foundation on which we establish our principles to live by. Faith is defined as "Complete trust or confidence in something for which there is no proof." More simply put, faith means believing that something is true, then committing our lives to it. Faith is the foundation on which people build principles by which to live. Faith is the foundation of Christianity. Scripture tells us that the way to God is through Jesus Christ. **"I am the way and the truth and the life. No one comes to the Father except through me" (John 14:6 NIV). "This righteousness is given through faith in Jesus Christ to all who believe" (Romans 3:22 NIV).**

The word "faith" is used 247 times in 231 verses in the King James Version (KJV). "Faith" is translated from the Greek root word "*pistis*," and "belief" from the verb form "*pisteuo*." The Greek words hold much more meaning than the English translations. "Faith" and "belief" are weaker words than the original meaning in Greek but are as close as we can get with English translation. We must make a conscious decision to put our faith in something greater than ourselves. This is an important step because there is more than one possibility from which to choose. We can choose to believe that God exists or doesn't. We can choose from many different religions. We can choose to believe that Christ is the path to God or some other path exists all together. I believe Christianity provides the correct path due to its beauty and simplicity and the equation $F = TL^3$ expresses that beauty and simplicity concisely.

"Faith" requires making a conscious choice. A choice as to what to trust in and how much to trust in it. Faith is rooted in trust. "T" represents the term "trust" and is the variable in this equation because trust is the basis of belief. Trust is intimately tied to the word "belief." Trust and belief are not mutually exclusive terms. In order for us to trust in something, we must believe it to be true. Conversely, in order to believe in something, we must have some level of trust in its truth as well. Trust in anything tends to vary from one moment to the next or one day to the next in response to our ever-changing circumstances. Our trust ebbs and flows like the tide giving us the feeling that our faith in God ebbs and flows as well. Trust fits so well as a term in this equation because a requirement for faith is trust. Therefore, trust is the variable in this equation. This is where the quality of our choice is controlled. We can either trust that God exists or we have to trust that God does not exist. Trust in the fullness of God's love and that God does exist would produce a greater value for faith in this equation. Trust that God does not love or does not exist would produce a vastly lower value for faith in this equation.

A person can control the amount of trust applied to the equation. The more trust we apply to the expression and multiply by it the constant "L" cubed, the stronger our faith becomes as illustrated in **Proverbs 3:5 NIV** (emphasis mine), **"Trust in the Lord with ALL your heart and lean not on your own understanding."** The word "all" implies the greatest possible value for the term "T" (trust). Trust is an integral part of this equation. Trust is defined as "A belief that someone or something is **true**, reliable, accurate, good, honest or effective." The word trust is mentioned 480 times in the KJV Bible. If we believe that God is true, good, reliable, honest, and accurate, then we would be remiss to hold back any amount of trust in God's love.

The Bible tells us to trust in God and not in ourselves or our plans or worldly things. Don't trust in the things that are temporary, perishable, and unstable. That will lead one toward death. Not death in the sense of being alive or dead but in the sense of eternal separation from God, a far more permanent state. **"Do not love the world or anything in the world. If anyone loves the world, love for the Father is not in them. For everything in the world—the lust of the flesh, the lust of the eyes, and the pride of life—comes not from the Father but from the world. The world and its desires pass away, but whoever does the will of God lives forever"** (1 John 2:15–17 NIV).

Now that we have explored the first two terms in the equation, faith and trust, let's look at "L" cubed, the constant in $F = TL^3$. Love is defined as an intense feeling of affection, fondness, tenderness, warmth, intimacy, endearment, adoration for someone or something; to adore, idolize, worship someone or something; to be unselfishly loyal and benevolent. The word love is mentioned approximately 348 times in the Bible and is inferred hundreds of other times.

Why make God's love, "L" cubed, the constant? Everything hinges on God's love. From the Old Testament to the New Testament. The whole Bible, including the Gospels, is an expression of God's infinite, limitless, and constant love for mankind. Without God's love, Jesus never comes to earth in the flesh, never dies on the cross to pay our debt of sin, and is never resurrected. But God does love us. **"For God so loved the world that he gave his one and only Son, that whoever believes in him shall not perish but have eternal life" (John 3:16 NIV).** The Bible is a love story. It is about God's love for us.

God's love is constant, infinite, and limitless. **"But you, Lord, are a compassionate and gracious God, slow to anger, abounding in love and faithfulness" (Psalm 86:15 NIV). "Give thanks to the God of heaven.** *His love endures forever"* **(Psalm 136:26 NIV).** $F = TL^3$ is anchored on the triune love of God—the love of the Father, of the Son, and of the Holy Spirit. This is the fullness of God's love represented in all three persons of God. **"But God, being rich in mercy, because of the great love with which he loved us" (Ephesians 2:4 ESV). "I live by faith in the Son of God, who loved me..." (Galatians 2:20 NIV). "God's love has been poured out into our hearts through the Holy Spirit, who has been given to us" (Romans 5:5 NIV).** God's love emanates from the Trinity, not just the Father or the Son but all three. "L^3" stands for the entirety of God's love. This love flows from God the Father, Jesus Christ the Son, and the Holy Spirit. This love is what all matter in the universe and all life in the universe is built on. Love is the defining factor of all things, as all that exist, exist because God loves.

Defining the term L^3 has been the most enlightening part of developing this expression. The love of God, Jesus, and the Holy Spirit is so profound and perfect that it is difficult to find the words to express it. The definition above just seems to fall short of what we truly experience when we experience the triune love of God. The words needed to express God's love, however, are found in the Bible. The Bible expresses God's love better than any other document in existence. There are approximately 3,116,480 letters used to make 783,137 words in 31,102 verses in 1,189 chapters in the 66 books of the Bible. The Bible has all the words that express God's love for mankind. It is a document that teaches us how to love God and Jesus by loving one another here on earth. We are called upon by God to love everyone, including our enemies. Love is the foundation of creation. Love is at the core of every man, woman, and child. People decay physically, mentally, and emotionally in the absence of love. Love is required to live a full, healthy life.

The power of the constant term "L^3" in this equation is breathtaking. One can see the difficulty in trying to express love in just a word or two. It really requires all 783,137 words of the Bible to properly express. The Bible expresses God's love very well. So, when we are determining the value we want to apply to our "T" (trust) in the "L^3" (love) of the Father, Son, and Holy Spirit, the Bible can give us a reference point to understand the power of "L^3" and that we must apply all our trust in it.

A love greater than any human being can ever imagine exists and is poured into each of us through the Holy Spirit. This love is evident in the Bible and in the world we experience every day. God has left it up to each of us to accept or reject it. God's love never diminishes because of our actions. God's love is ever present in our lives through our ups and downs, through our sins and suffering.

The equation $F = TL^3$ can be used as a tool to reflect and pray on our own faith. It can be a tool to start conversations with others. We can use it to tell others about what our relationship with Jesus Christ means to us. It can help us strengthen our own faith and to go and make disciples of others.

CHAPTER 3

TRUTH

"For God so loved the world that he gave his one and only Son, that whoever believes in him shall not perish but have eternal life."
(JOHN 3:16 NIV)

B efore we can use the equation $F = TL^3$ as a tool to help us disciple others, we first have to understand how it fits into Christianity and points us to accepting Jesus Christ as our savior. So let's look more closely at the constant term L^3 in this equation. If a person is going to place their trust in anything, that person would want to fully know that it is "truth" that they are placing their trust in. As we read earlier, the Bible is a book about God's love for all of us. The Gospels are a culmination of that love, a pinnacle act of love for mankind. The word "Gospel" means "good news." There are four Gospels written in the New Testament. The four Gospels are accounts of Jesus' birth, life, death, and resurrection. The four Gospels are attributed to the authors Matthew, Mark, Luke, and John and each provide their own perspective of Jesus' story.

Jesus, the only begotten Son of God, comes to earth to be tortured and killed in one of the most brutal forms of execution in human history for the sole purpose of paying the ultimate debt of sin, saving all people from an eternal separation from God so we may all *live* and is then resurrected three days later defeating death. All we, here on earth, have to do is simply accept that as *truth*.

Faith is the cornerstone of how we live our lives. Christians, Muslims, Hindus, and even atheists all develop a foundation of principles on which to build their lives from their faith. From this foundation, people typically make all their life's choices, from personal to financial and everything in between. People determine how to react to circumstances and how to treat others based on their principles. That is why it is so important to develop your faith on the belief in and trusting of what would be the most constant, rock solid of truths. If the foundation of your faith is uncertain and shaky, then your life will be uncertain and shaky. If your faith is rooted in sound unfailing truth, your life will be rooted in sound unfailing truth.

This book is not going to debate the historical accuracy or specific events in the Bible. I will leave those debates and arguments about the factual content, the historicity of biblical events, and the defense of those specific to the school of apologetics. Apologists Ravi Zacharias, J. P. Moreland, Lee Strobel, Gary Habermas, Nabeel Qureshi, Stephen Myer, and many more have performed the forensic investigations and documented the defenses that support the historical accuracy of the Bible. They have done this work very successfully. So, as I stated, for the purposes of this text, I am not going to appeal to the Bible's historical accuracy. I, instead, want to appeal to the reader's intuition.

Now, let's focus on God's love as truth. How do we know that God's love is true and represents complete truth? The answer is right in front of us. Love is the ultimate expression of truth. We all know this to be true. We don't need a PhD in philosophy or theology to understand this. We all know this intuitively. Think of your own love. Do you love your children? For most, the answer is, of course, *yes*. So ask yourself, how true is your love for your children? If you are like me, it is very true. Nothing could be truer. Barring severe mental illness, no one has ever said "I love my children, but that is not really true." Even when our kids misbehave and drive us crazy, we still love them. A parent's love for a child is true and represents absolute truth. How about our spouse or significant other?

Do we love them "but not really?" Of course not. You love them and you know it to be true. You can put family or friends in the sentence "I love my...." We truly love the people we love. Why do you think we call it "true love?" Because love is true, love is truth. As a matter of fact, "false love" doesn't even exist as false love isn't love at all. It is something else altogether. Perhaps it is hate, jealousy, anger, or disdain for another, but it is not love. Love is the ultimate expression of truth.

The Bible tells us that God loves us like a father loves his children. Jesus refers to God as Father, both his Father and our Father. God's love for us, in fact, is far greater than parental love. **"If you then, who are evil, know how to give good gifts to your children, how much more will the heavenly Father give the Holy Spirit to those who ask him!" (Luke 11:13 ESV).**

We know our love represents complete truth, and if God's love is even greater than our own, we have to realize this is the greatest of all truths. **"Greater love has no one than this, that someone lay down his life for his friends" (John 15:13 ESV).**

We know we are experiencing the deepest, most meaningful expression of love when we put our love into action. Putting love into action is when love becomes sacrificial. When we do things, anything for those we love, love becomes sacrificial. Whenever you do something for another, you give up, you sacrifice the opportunity to do for yourself. Maybe we sacrifice just a little, or we are completely willing to sacrifice everything including our own life for those we love. Nevertheless, giving up the opportunity to do for yourself, whether small or great, is sacrifice. As parents, we sacrifice so much for the love of our children. As husbands and wives, we sacrifice so much for our spouse. Most people would even lay down their lives for their kids or spouse. There are countless stories of people sacrificing themselves for their children, for their spouse, for a friend, and even for a stranger. These are examples of deep meaningful love. There is no greater truth than a love that is expressed by the sacrificing of one's own life. We see this in John 15:13. This is also what Jesus did for you and me. Jesus sacrificed his own life to save ours. Jesus died on the cross so we may live.

We know love is true. We also understand that true love is sacrificial.

God's love is true love because he sacrificed so much for his love for us. He came to earth in the form of his only Son, and he died on the cross so we all may live. This is why I can accept Jesus as my savior. Because the Gospel is rooted in God's true sacrificial love for me; it is rooted in truth and my faith is a product of that truth. So I pray every day, *"Father give me the wisdom to place ALL my Trust in your love because you loved me so much you were willing to die for me so I may live. Thank you, Father, for your unfailing love."* As I stated earlier, it *all* hinges on God's love for us. Without God's love, perhaps creation never happens. Without God's love, mankind would never be pursued and Jesus would never have come to save us. It is all a product of God's love for you and me.

Since we are appointing the term L^3 or the triune love of God as the constant in this equation, we can be certain that the term "trust" is being applied to truth because God's love is truth. We now know that, if we place *all* our trust in the love of the Father, the Son, and the Holy Spirit, we are placing our trust in something that is true and is, in fact, truth. We can also see that God is true and that Jesus is true. There is nothing that represents a greater truth.

By what authority do we know this? We know this by God's written authority—the Bible. So then, how do we know the Bible is true and represents truth? The first and most important step is to read the Bible for yourself. You can't make an informed opinion without actually reading the Word of God. If you haven't read the Bible, then the points that follow are just some author's opinions that hold no real context for the reader. If you don't know where to start, start from the beginning. Open a Bible and start with Genesis 1:1. Some people recommend you start with the Gospel of John or Matthew. It doesn't really matter where you start as long as you just open the Bible and start reading. You will soon see that the Bible is a love story. A story of God's love for you and me.

You may not fully understand everything you read in the Bible at first. There are many resources you can refer to in order to help you understand. I personally like to reach out to other Christians who have been in the Word for many years. I enjoy asking questions and hearing their interpretations. It is important to look to several resources as people interpret the Bible a little differently from one another. This doesn't necessarily make any one interpretation wrong, just different. Listen to several interpretations and go with what you feel is most accurate. Sometimes you will even see it a little differently yourself and develop your own interpretation, and that is perfectly okay.

The Bible is the authority by which we know God loves us. If the Bible is God's expression of his love for us and we know that love is truth, we can then assign truth to the Bible itself. The overarching concept that the Bible represents God's unwavering constant love for you and me proves conceptually that the Bible must then at its very core represent truth. Love cannot be false because false love isn't love at all. As mentioned above, the Bible is a love story, a very unique love story. It is about God's love for us. An amazing and beautiful aspect of the Bible is that you and I, the readers of the Bible, are the object of the love represented in the Bible—God's love. We the readers are the object of all the love expressed in all sixty-six books of the Bible. When we read traditional love stories, the object of the love expressed in the story is just another character in the story. For example, in Shakespeare's *Romeo and Juliet*, the object of Romeo's love is Juliet and the object of Juliet's love is Romeo. In the Bible, however, you and I are the object of the love—God's love. This gives the Bible a very unique and beautiful perspective.

The next point I would like to make as I appeal to your intuition is the brutal honesty and transparency of the Bible. The Bible airs mankind's dirtiest laundry. Throughout the Bible, we read about lying, cheating, deceiving, adultery, violence, murder, rape, incest, and failure after failure. We read that following Christ will lead to attacks and persecution. If early Christians wanted to contrive or "make up" a wild story that was designed to get you to follow them, give up a lot of what you believed, and alter your very culture...don't you think they would have painted a prettier picture? A picture that doesn't remind us of our brokenness and failures? A picture that doesn't result in opposition, persecution, and your possible murder? A picture that would simply be easier to accept?

In the Bible, God doesn't promise us that we will no longer experience heartache and pain here on earth. The apostles and early Christians were persecuted. They were tortured, jailed, and even murdered. Following Christ has been, throughout history, a very dangerous proposition. This isn't necessarily a band of people I would want to follow based on the writings in the Bible if the Bible was false. However, we can be comfortable knowing the Bible represents complete truth. Christians throughout history knew something…something to be so true that not even the fear of persecution and death could keep them from it. That truth is something I can get behind.

Take the story of Paul and his contribution to Christianity. Paul was a well-educated citizen of Rome and Jewish leader, a Pharisee who violently persecuted early Christians. After encountering the resurrected Jesus on the road to Damascus, the apostle Paul dedicated his life to following Christ. Paul gave up everything to do this. He was a respected leader in Jewish society and could have had great material wealth as a result. Paul, however, chose to follow Jesus after experiencing Christ's truth—Christ's love—and he risked his life many times over to pursue that truth. Truth is powerful and beautiful. Only truth could account for what the apostles, early Christians, and contemporary Christians alike risked and continue to this day to risk life and limb for. If this story was just a fabrication, why include it? Why tell a story about a man who had what appeared to be everything only to give it up to be beaten, imprisoned, shipwrecked, bitten by poisonous snakes, and ultimately killed for following Jesus Christ? There are dozens of stories like this in both the Old and New Testaments of the Bible. It doesn't follow any logic to include these stories unless they were true.

This honesty and transparency lend to the credibility and truth of the Bible because it is simply not in our nature to be that brutally honest. If you don't believe that, then just read the social media posts of you and your connections. When we look closely at social media posts, we are typically only shown the very best side of the people posting about themselves. People rarely post a tainted picture of themselves. We just get a highlight reel of people's successes and victories. When we take a picture of ourselves, we pose with what we believe to be our best side forward. The honesty and transparency of the Bible are too raw to not represent truth. God inspired men to write the words in the Bible because that is what is true. Like it or not, there is a picture of mankind's ugly truth in the Bible. God cannot lie and therefore only inspires truth. It is up to us to accept it or not and that is part of God's design for "free will" and for love. I will discuss free will and love in great detail in later chapters.

As I read the Bible, I sometimes feel as though I am reading mankind's confession of all that is wrong with humanity. A confession is an admittance of guilt. Typically, people don't confess lies. Certainly not that many people as there are authors represented in the Bible, authors who are separated in time by hundreds and even a few thousand years. When we confess, we pour out our honest truths. A false confession would just be an attempt to conceal the truth and wouldn't be a real confession at all. The authors of the Bible were inspired by God to confess not just to God but to all readers of the Bible the honest, transparent profession of who and what we are as human beings. This is the truth. If we are to trust truth as a foundation for our faith, then the Bible has to represent truth in order for us to have a secure, rock solid basis for our principles. There is simply no other explanation. Mankind is just not capable of that kind of honesty. If the Bible were false and written by man alone, it would glorify man not God. The Bible clearly glorifies God.

The equation $F = TL^3$ brings us to Jesus. How? Placing all your trust in the triune love of God strengthens your faith and strengthens your relationship with God. Knowing and trusting just how much God loves you will give you the insight that the Gospel is true as it is also an expression of love. Since true love is sacrificial and we know Jesus willingly died for us out of his love for us, it makes complete sense to trust that love, to trust that truth. As we read earlier in this chapter, it is all about Jesus. Placing all your trust in the same love that caused God to send his only begotten Son to die for our sins and be raised is a natural step to accepting Jesus. You can accept Jesus as your savior because his entire existence is rooted in God's sacrificial love and, as a result, is rooted in complete truth.

The Bible also tells us that God is love. **"Anyone who does not love does not know God, because God is love" (1 John 4:8 ESV). "God is love, and whoever abides in love abides in God, and God abides in him" (1 John 4:16 ESV).** So, by placing all our trust in the triune love of God, we are also placing all our trust in the three persons of God himself—the Father, Son, and Holy Spirit. By trusting in God's love, we are actually trusting in God. Throughout the book, I may interchange God's love with just God because God is love. And if God is love, then Jesus is God's greatest expression of love because Jesus represents God's sacrificial love. So, if we understand that it *all* hinges on God's greatest expression of love, then we can see that it *all* hinges on Jesus. It is truly all about Jesus. When we trust in God's love, we are also trusting in Jesus. This logic completely reinforces our need to accept Jesus as our Lord and savior.

Accepting this truth and proclaiming Jesus *will* change your life—it won't necessarily change your circumstances immediately, but if you sit still and listen intently, you will hear God's instructions for changing your circumstances. God will speak change into you. I have had people tell me "that just seems too hard to do." It can be difficult. God makes no promises that it will be easy. After all, was it too hard for God to send his only Son to die a brutal death on the cross? Was it too hard for Jesus to endure the pain of ridicule, torture, and being nailed to a cross until he suffocated to death? Was it too hard to make such a loving sacrifice just so you and I may live? I would say it was the most difficult act in all of human history made easy because God loves us so much. I think if Jesus can make that big of a sacrifice for us, we can take the time to listen and follow his instructions for our lives no matter how hard we think that might be. The peace, joy, and sense of comfort that comes from following God's plan for us is truly liberating.

CHAPTER 4

A LEARNING PROCESS

"I am the way and the truth and the life, no one comes to the Father but through me."

(JOHN 14:6 NIV)

Having concluded that placing all our trust in the triune love of God leads us to the logical next step of accepting Jesus as our one and only savior, our true path to God, we must now determine how we use this as a tool to perhaps find or just reaffirm our faith each and every day.

As I pray each day, I meditate on my faith. I ask God to give me the strength and wisdom to put *all* my trust in his love, the fullness of his love. That means the love of the Father, the Son, and the Holy Spirit. By fully placing all my trust in that love, I can understand why God sent his only begotten Son…it was out of his love for us. Because it was from his love that he sent the Son, I can accept Jesus Christ as my savior and as truth.

Ask God every day for the strength and wisdom to place your trust in his love (L^3). It is the foundation of your faith and a steadfast, infinite, limitless, and constant foundation to live your life on. You don't have to replace your traditional prayers during your personal time with God, but you can add it to your list of prayers. It is short and concise and will help to illustrate your relationship with God.

Reaffirming our relationship with Jesus each and every day is an important part of our Christian life. After all, life is very complicated, people are very complicated. Satan is constantly on the attack. It is easy to forget God's love and believe that we as individuals are in complete control of our lives without any divine intervention. We all have wants and desires and they don't always coincide with God's plan for our lives. As a result, we tend to listen to the voice of the enemy and believe God has left us in our season of struggles and suffering. Nothing could be farther from the truth. God's love is limitless. God's Love never diminishes and never leaves us no matter how bad we mess up, no matter how bad we sin. Jesus paid the ultimate debt out of pure love. God's love is the most constant, unwavering truth in the universe. This is why it is so important to remind ourselves every day of just how much God loves us and that he will never leave us. Writing this equation, $F = TL^3$, on little notes around your house, on your bathroom mirror, or on your front door so you see it every time you get ready in the morning or leave the house is a good way to remind yourself of God's love for you.

I ultimately found my faith during a very difficult season and spent several years reaffirming and growing that faith through prayer, reading, and eventually finding this equation. Many years ago, I went through a very difficult divorce. A divorce that should have lasted six to twelve months went on for over three and a half years. To add insult to injury during the divorce, I was falsely accused of molesting my youngest child. My daughter was coached on just what to say to teachers and the Homeroom moms. My little princess was being driven away from me. The psychological, emotional, and financial stress was almost unbearable. Parents at my daughter's school looked at me with disdain. I had to hire a criminal defense attorney and psychiatric professionals to assist in the case which added tens of thousands of dollars to the total cost of the divorce. I was being attacked daily with venomous intentions. To make matters worse, I was diagnosed with cancer in the midst of all this turmoil. Emotionally and psychologically, I was a wreck. The levels of fear and anxiety that plagued me in that season would be enough to drive most men to take drastic measures. At the time, I hadn't accepted Jesus Christ as my savior and I wasn't sure I even believed in God. After all, what God would allow all this to happen to one person all at one time? This question will be answered in later chapters. Who could be strong enough to survive that much stress, emotional pain, anxiety, and fear? With God's love supporting me through it all, I was made strong enough even though I was unaware of that love at that moment.

Looking back many years later, I realized I wasn't alone. I did not know it at the time but God was always there giving me strength and pursuing me with all his love. As the divorce unfolded and the experts determined the truth of my innocence, things got better for me and my children. I was granted full custody of our children for almost two years. Financially, my situation improved. I bought a house and moved to a quiet neighborhood. My kids recovered from the drama and abuse they endured through a long and painful divorce. My ex-wife and I were eventually able to share custody again after some time.

Here is the curious thing—as everything in my life seemed to be improving, I found myself questioning why. Why did it all happen? It was the questioning that led me to answers I did not expect. I started attending church at this point in my life and I realized that God allowed these events to take place so I could be prepared for the next season in my life. God was refining me so I could handle with a newfound wisdom what I had to do next. I had to come to forgive my ex-wife for all that transpired. This was very difficult but I have forgiven her. It didn't happen overnight either. As my faith has increased, my ability to forgive increased as well. I began to understand the nature of God's love and what it means to truly love and be loved. This made it possible to forgive an almost unforgivable act. The act of being falsely accused of molesting your children just for money.

My ex-wife and I went through a very difficult season and we were not very pleasant to each other. But as sure as I write these words on this page, I have forgiven her. Because as I prayed over the equation $F = TL^3$, I began to see how God's love for me allowed for his forgiveness of my sins. Forgiveness is a product of love. For me to truly forgive my ex-wife, I had to develop a love for her as well. How could I love a woman whom I had gone through a supremely difficult divorce with? That was a strength I could only receive through Jesus Christ. If God could forgive me for my sins, then how could I not forgive my ex-wife? How could I come to any other outcome but loving and forgiving her? I couldn't. There really is no other way. I do wish I had this equation as I went through those difficult years. It would have given me peace in a time I felt none.

As for the cancer, that was a pivotal point in my coming to Jesus. When I was diagnosed, my daughter was six years old and my son was twelve. I found myself researching the survivability of my disease and started calculating what age my kids would be when I might die as a result of the cancer. I wanted to give them the best possible environment—knowing their mother was not well psychologically—for as long as I could to give them the best chance of a normal childhood before I died. In the three months following my diagnosis, I told my family, friends, and coworkers about my cancer. The people I loved the most were quietly placing me on prayer chains at their churches and other religious organizations. I even had a team of Portuguese mothers baking me prayer breads. I had calculated that the total number of people praying for me exceeded 70,000. Seventy thousand strangers praying for a stranger to be healed. My heart was opening to new ideas.

In April of 2012, I went through a lengthy surgery with family and friends by my side. The surgeon said that the surgery went well and thought that they got it all, but wouldn't be certain until the results came back from pathology. I was scheduled to see my oncologist two weeks after I was discharged from the hospital. A few days prior to my follow up appointment, the oncologist called and postponed my appointment without explanation. That was unnerving.

A week later, I did have my follow-up appointment. At the meeting, my doctor explained that he had to send my tumor off to several independent pathologists to get the most accurate result possible. He then explained that the cancerous tumor had been completely encapsulated in benign tissue. He had to make sure the margins of the benign tissue had no evidence of the cancerous tumor breaching the mass. He concluded as did all the pathologists that the cancer did not breach the benign tissue and I was completely healed. The doctor had no explanation for this and assured me that he had never seen anything like it.

Well, I did have an explanation and it was prayer. It was as if God had reached in and cupped the tumor with his own hands, protecting me from the cancer and healing me in the process. I immediately felt the love of God flowing through me. I was filled with so much joy I could hardly stand it. I believe God knew I needed to be in my children's lives for the long term. I experienced a medical miracle through God, but he also had to prepare me for the difficult task of forgiving the mother of my children to be a positive example to her and to them. God's love was pouring into me and I was beginning to fully trust that love. I was officially on a mission to know God.

Two years later in 2014, God placed on my heart the equation $F = TL^3$. I used it to continue to develop my relationship with God and continue to pursue Jesus. I started attending Limitless Church regularly. I started serving every week and even joined several small groups. On April 10th, 2016, my pastor and friend Matt Blair of Limitless Church in Tampa, Florida baptized me in the name of the Father, Son, and Holy Spirit. I fully and publicly declared my life to Jesus Christ that day.

Meditating on this equation for two full years helped me to strengthen my faith and develop a closer relationship with God. I continue to do so every day and find myself reaffirming my faith when it weakens. The flesh is weak. Our earthly desires can distract us from what is most important. Now, I am most certainly not telling you to not want things in life. I am saying, put those things in perspective because God will provide. God loves us so much that he wants us to be happy. By placing our trust in his love, we can give it all over to him and allow him to provide for us.

I went through a very difficult season, and even though I wanted provision when I wanted it, God provided at just the right time for the best outcome for me and my life. God always came through even though, perhaps, I wished it was sooner. Looking back, it is easy to see that the timing was always perfect because it was God's timing. It all came together in the development of the equation $F = TL^3$.

"I have told you these things, so that in me you may have peace. In this world you will have trouble. But take heart!"
(John 16:33 NIV)

We will all experience hardship in life which can lead to worry, fear, and anxiety. Anxiety can be debilitating. When we find ourselves in the greatest state of anxiety, we are typically as far from God as we can be. We begin to put everything on our own shoulders and believe that there is no way out because we can't see a way out. We believe that we alone have to solve the dilemma or there will be no resolution and we will never escape our circumstances. That is when we are most vulnerable to believing the lies that cripple us with fear. That is also the time when we must remember God's love and God's promise. Just because you think God has abandoned you, he hasn't.

By focusing on the equation $F = TL^3$, we can pray about putting all our trust in God's love. When we place our trust in his love, we can see that God is there and he has not abandoned us. We can put the fear and anxiety on him knowing "God has this," God will provide. By doing this, our fear and anxiety can melt away. It is so simple, however, it is not easy. We are weak and broken. We will pull away from God when times are tough but God pursues. Think about trusting God's love and pray about it. In so doing, your faith will be restored, your fear and anxiety will disappear. It does, however, take time and practice. I have been meditating and praying on this equation for several years, and each time, it gets a little bit easier and the fear dissipates a little faster every time. I pray over $F = TL^3$, putting as much trust as I can into the constant unwavering triune love of God.

It doesn't matter what is troubling me, I can always find peace by praying over this one simple equation and using it to focus in on Jesus.

Financial matters, matters of the heart, health-related matters, issues of personal appearance, issues with my children, or issues at work always seem less daunting when basking in the glory of God's love. You also can find peace and strengthened faith when you place all our trust in the triune love of God. I am sure it would have been much easier on me when I went through those dark times if I understood this then, but I am content looking back knowing God was there with me and that he did love me. Perhaps that prepared me to develop this equation that I use now and share with you today.

Another way to use the equation $F = TL^3$ is during arguments. If you are like me when in the heat of an argument, I always seem to place my full trust in my side of the argument. I know I am right and no one can pull me down from that stance. So, as a way to reset myself, I pray over this equation. For example, when I am in a heated argument with my wife, I find myself trusting in my points as being the right points. By stopping and apologizing to my wife, I simply say: "I am sorry, honey. I am putting so much trust in my side of this argument that it isn't allowing me to see your side objectively. Let's put our trust in God's love for us and pray on that. Perhaps that will help us better understand each other's point." This exercise has been wildly successful in my marriage. We come together on most issues as a result of resetting the argument by praying over placing our full trust in God's love, knowing that God has the answer for us. We just have to trust him and listen to him. This has also brought us closer together. By allowing our faith to grow together by choosing to place our trust in God's love, it allows us to let more of God's love flow into each of us. That love naturally flows through us and into each other. Working with and praying through this equation has had wonderful results in our relationship.

Meditating and praying on this equation helps me every day and I believe it can do the same for you. No matter where you are in your faith, I pray this equation helps you daily as a simple expression of your faith in Jesus Christ. It is effortless to think about and contemplate $F = TL^3$ as it is only three terms. It is not complicated and provides a great deal of peace—peace in knowing and trusting how much God loves you and understanding the sacrifice he made for each of you.

Let's look at what we have covered. Faith is a foundational aspect of everyone's life regardless of the placement of faith. Christianity, Judaism, Islam, Hinduism, Buddhism, and even atheism are all based on faith. Everyone, regardless of religion, puts their trust in something they believe to be true. That is what forms the basis of their faith. Because faith is any individual's foundation for life, for the choices they make, for the way they treat others, and really for every aspect of daily life, it is imperative to place the framework of trust entirely on truth. Believe in and trust truth. God's love is constant, infinite, unwavering, limitless, and true. We know this because intuitively, we know that love is truth. No one has ever experienced untrue love, only true love. Despite there being varying degrees of love, sacrificial love is the love of a father, a mother, a spouse, or a friend. Being willing to sacrifice everything, even life itself for another, shows no greater love.

God spent thousands of years lovingly pursuing his people only to be rejected time and time again. Finally, we read in the Gospels God, once and for all, proves his love for us by coming down to earth in the form of a Son, and with an expression of no greater love, sacrificed his life so we may live. So that you and I, each and every one of us, may live. By understanding the extent of God's love for us, we can see the truth in Jesus Christ and know that our faith in this truth allows us to easily accept Jesus Christ as our true savior. The equation $F = TL^3$ can remind us daily of the extent of God's love for us and can remind us of the price God paid, the blood Jesus shed for our salvation. *Wow*, that is a truth I can place the full extent of my trust in. This truth is what God placed on my heart when I developed the equation $F = TL^3$.

By praying over this equation, by using this illustration to pursue God's love each and every day, making it a part of our prayer time—our time with God—we can use this equation as a tool to help us through all the trouble this world can throw at us. We can use the equation in times of prosperity to remind ourselves that God is responsible and God should be thanked and praised and worshiped. This will keep our relationship right with God.

There are many examples of God's love completely changing people's lives. In this next chapter, I will explore several personal testimonies of people who have been transformed by God's love. They were able to overcome adversity, find healing (both mental and physical), and see the light once again from a place of deep darkness. They found Jesus Christ through complete trust in God's steadfast love.

CHAPTER 5

WE ARE NOT ALONE IN THIS

"Therefore do not be ashamed of the testimony about our Lord, nor of me his prisoner, but share in suffering for the gospel by the power of God..."

(2 TIMOTHY 1:8 ESV)

Hearing accounts of others who have had their lives transformed through the triune love of God gives us real life examples to associate with. This is important because people need to know they are not alone in their struggles. Others are experiencing the same difficulties, fears, anxieties, worries, and doubts. God knows what people are experiencing. God is actively transforming every day the lives of those who sit still and just listen. **"Come and hear, all you who fear God, and I will tell what he has done for my soul" (Psalm 66:16 ESV).**

As you will see in the following testimonies, God took time to prepare each individual for his purpose for them. Today's society is very fast paced. We expect results immediately and have lost patience with anything less than that immediacy. We want what we want when we want it and not later. That is just not necessarily God's timing. We have to remind ourselves that God's timing is perfect. In the moment, it is hard to wait for God's timing, but the outcome is always better than we could ever imagine.

Let's Meet Jon

Jon is a good friend of mine in his late twenties and since he was about seventeen years old, he has struggled with anxiety and depression. Jon's story is one of courage and perseverance through the darkest of times. After high school, Jon's parents divorced; he dropped out of college. Anyone who knows Jon would find that to be out of character for him. He is a studious, intelligent young man who enjoys writing poetry and has a very creative mind. Dropping out of college would not have been what I would expect from him. However, anxiety and depression have a funny way of getting people to fall out of character. It wasn't long before he found himself sleeping in his car on most nights with an occasional invite to crash on the couch of a friend or two from time to time. A great feeling of hopelessness began to get its grip on him and he felt as if he had no direction and nowhere to turn.

Despite dropping out of college, John was not a quitter. He was not ready to give up on his life. He knew he had worth and something to offer the world, so John joined the Army. Perhaps the discipline of a military career could help him find the direction he felt he had lost. John found that life in the Army came pretty easy; after all, the army trained him to follow orders, a relatively easy task for someone of above average intelligence. Jon became enamored with the idea of fighting in combat for his country. He was being given the skills and tools to do just that. The Army trained him to kill. John worked very hard at accomplishing all the Army asked of him and he was very good at it. A great sense of pride came over him when he imagined being in combat. *That is where heroes are made,* he thought. What could be greater than risking one's life for the liberty and freedom of his fellow Americans back home? The whole idea gave Jon a feeling of being renewed and once again having a purpose. Jon, however, was never deployed into battle. His feeling of being renewed quickly turned into a renewed sense of being lost again. Anxiety and depression began to rear their ugly heads once more and filled him with that gut-wrenching hopelessness.

There was a strength in Jon. A strength that kept him moving forward, swimming against a powerful current flowing from a sea of recurring depression and anxiety. The toll taken on his mental health was high, but Jon found a way to dig deep within himself. Jon could always dig past the facade anxiety and depression placed on his mind as to who he was. Even after losing everything he owned in a fire and a failed and very toxic relationship, Jon persevered. Yes, he was lonely and depressed and despite looking for an escape hatch which he found in alcohol and gambling at the time; he was soon reminded of a childhood desire to be an Air Force pilot. Jon spent the next several years putting all he had into that dream. Jon's dream. He went back to school and joined the Air Force ROTC program at the university to be a pilot. But God had a way of letting him know that those plans were not the plans God had for him. Jon put much effort into a relationship that was outside of God's plan and he worked even harder for a career that also fell outside of God's plan for him. So when the day came and he received the letter telling him he was going to be an Air Force pilot, he felt completely empty. No joy, no sense of fulfillment. None of Jon's problems went away with the news of getting his dream job. Jon found this frame of mind to be very confusing and believed something was very wrong with himself. Mental illness can do that to a person.

Jon started drowning himself again in alcohol and behaved in a self-destructive manner. It was as if he was trying to sabotage his new-found career himself. In these times of weakness, the enemy will come calling. It was Satan whispering in his ear putting thoughts of suicide in his head. Satan wants to destroy. The enemy wants you to believe you are all alone, whispering, "No one cares about you, not your family, not friends." Jon knew deep down inside those were lies and that he wasn't alone. Jon thought to himself, *No one? Really? Not even you, God?* It was in that moment he shook off the lies and looked to God. He prayed for

God's love and for God to be with him in this darkest of moments. He prayed, "God I need you." God had been by Jon's side all those years, but Jon was so focused on what "Jon wanted," on the career Jon wanted, the relationship Jon wanted that he was blinded to what God had planned for him. He was blinded to God's ever-present love. After all those years of pulling away from God, as soon as he turned and looked up to God, God answered, "I am here. I have always been here. I love you."

Jon felt such a tremendous love, the love of God that led to a deep desire to reflect that love onto others. Jon decided to start serving at Limitless Church, a church he had attended off and on for a while He served in the Children's Ministry. He would soon learn that this is where he was needed and loved. The director of the Children's Ministry stopped Jon after services one day and told him how she had been praying for a man to help out as the boys needed a role model. She regularly gives Jon a hug and tells him he is such a blessing.

A few weeks later, Pastor Matt Blair asked if Jon would testify to the whole congregation his story. A story of struggling with mental illness. Jon agreed to testify to the congregation even though it could jeopardize his career as a pilot. Jon was brave and felt overwhelming freedom on the platform that day. He received a standing ovation after his talk. It was a powerful and enlightening message. I know because I was there in the audience. After services, he was approached by many with "me too moments." People wanted to talk to Jon about their own stories and let him know he is not alone. Pastor Matt even told him several months later that someone had walked into church struggling with depression and thoughts of suicide. It was the direct result of hearing Jon's talk that morning that prompted this person to reach out for help. Jon's courage to share his pain and struggles has saved lives. God placed Jon in just the right place to make a profound difference in the life of another. Jon finally started down the long path to healing through God's love.

Jon was eventually notified that his commission for the Air Force was denied. His "dream job" was gone. Jon will tell you, though, that he is perfectly content with that. He has God's love and now listens closely to what God has planned for his future. He has hope and a deep feeling of joy about God's plans for him.

Jon still struggles. The path toward healing takes time and effort. Jon is a man who has seen the power of God's love in his life. Through the strength God has granted him, Jon reflects God's love onto those around him, and for that, I and many others are eternally grateful. Jon is a blessing to many. His friendship has had a profound impact on my life as well as the lives of my family. I simply can't imagine a world without Jon in it.

I find Jon's story very relatable. We all have lives that are spotted with poor decisions and a little bad luck. It is perfectly normal to experience these things in life. When struggling with mental health issues just below the surface, just outside of other's awareness, these very struggles can be eclipsing. It takes God's steadfast, unfailing love to pull you out of these situations regardless of your condition. I asked Jon recently, "What did God's love have to do with his healing and direction for the future?" Jon replied, "Everything!"

Jon published his story on the website "Thisismybrave.com," a site dedicated to ending stigmas associated with mental illness, creating an open forum where people can speak freely on the topic and begin the journey toward healing.

Let's Meet Jenny

Jenny has been a colleague of mine for several years. Twenty years ago when Jenny was only in her early twenties, she was diagnosed with having a major ischemic stroke. An ischemic stroke occurs when an artery to the brain is blocked. The brain depends on its arteries to bring fresh oxygen-rich and nutrient-rich blood from the heart and lungs. The blood then carries away carbon dioxide and cellular waste. When the arteries are blocked, this process can't take place. This will cause the brain cells to slow the production of energy and eventually stop altogether. If the arteries remain blocked even for only a few minutes, brain cells can start to die.

At the time of her stroke, Jenny had all of the hopes and dreams of any young woman in her early twenties. That all changed in an instant. Jenny started behaving strangely and slurring her speech at work one morning. Her boss knew something was wrong and called 911. She was admitted into the hospital, and that night while in her hospital room, she had a stroke. When Jenny regained consciousness in the hospital the next morning, she learned that the traumatic brain injury caused by the stroke left her unable to walk, move her hands and arms, and unable to speak. She also suffered from aphasia. Aphasia is caused by brain cell damage to the areas of the brain responsible for speech. It can result in the inability to form words and sentences, causing difficulty in communicating.

Jenny spent the next month in the hospital where she started physical, occupational, and speech therapy. There were hours of painful exercises to help her regain her strength. One day while being transported to her room via her wheelchair, she remembered a nurse saying, "Poor girl, doesn't look like she will ever recover." Jenny was unable to respond, nonetheless, she wasn't deterred by the comment. She was determined to recover 100% functionality because Jesus Christ had already paid the price for her healing! After a month in the hospital, Jenny was released to outpatient therapy to regain her ability to walk and speak. For the next year, she endured extensive physical, occupational, and speech therapy. She went from being wheelchair-bound to using a cane to assist her with walking. It would be about a year and a half before her back and legs were strong enough for her to be able to walk on her own without the use of a cane.

Jenny had to use a communication binder to communicate with her family and friends. The communication binder included some of her therapy exercises with the words "yes" or "no" as well as the alphabet on the front cover. With her fingers, she would point to "yes" or "no" to provide an answer to a question or the alphabet to create sentences. After a full year of speech therapy, she was able to regain her ability to speak. What was most impressive about the following year was Jenny actually completed her college requirements and graduated while going through her recovery process. She says God was at work in her that year and she was given great strength to accomplish all that she has accomplished. When Jenny was released from the hospital, she was unable to live alone at the time and moved back in with her mom.

Growing up, Jenny attended church regularly on Sundays, but when she moved out of her mom's apartment, she began to live a life that drew her attention away from church and God. After moving back in with her mom, she began to attend church again on a regular basis. As time progressed, Jenny began to realize how much grace and love God placed in her throughout her recovery. Like many people, Jenny was not aware of what God was doing in the moment. Eventually, with prayer and reflection, it became very evident.

Twenty years later, Jenny is left with a slight limp and opportunities for improvement in the areas of communication that are still being strengthened today with the wisdom and revelation of the Holy Spirit. Jenny currently works as a sales analyst and gives God all of the glory for the ability to progress rather than regress in her career path. She passed the Florida State Insurance Licensing, an accomplishment she is particularly proud of. Jenny is also engaged to be married to a wonderful and patient man who loves her very much. She attributes her remarkable recovery to God's steadfast love for her.

Jenny could have followed any path after her stroke. She could have given up and followed a path of anger and self-pity. A path that more than likely would have led to a life of despair and dependency on others. Jenny, however, chose to follow the path of God's love and healing. A path that has led to a life reliant on God, of freedom, and confidence in the name of Jesus Christ.

The enemy will try to destroy your relationship with God. He will place challenges and hurdles in front of you that are designed to break your spirit and drive you away from Jesus. You have a choice, though. You have free will. Jenny could have turned from God in anger and self-pity. She could have given up. When God put courage and perseverance on her heart, she grabbed on to it and held on to it as if her life depended on it. Her life did depend on it. Jenny chose to trust in God's love for her.

After twenty years, she continues to trust in God's love. She chooses to allow God's love to lift up her spirit rather than let Satan's lies drag her down into despair, fear, anger, and self-pity. Jenny chooses love. The path she took was most definitely the more difficult path. Satan makes his path look easy. That is how he gets you. Today, Jenny is a vibrant, intelligent, and beautiful woman of God despite the challenges of everyday life!

Jenny refuses to let the enemy take her. She has a smile that lights up a room. That light emanates from the joy of the Holy Spirit that pours into her every day. With the help of the Holy Spirit, she affirms that today, she's got more wisdom and revelation than ever before. She declares, "I can do *all* things through Christ who strengthens me," and "I can do nothing without my Papa God, my beloved Jesus Christ, and my wisdom and revelation—the Holy Spirit!" Jenny proclaims, "My faith, love, and trust in the Lord our God is stronger. Every day, I live to be an ambassador for Jesus Christ!"

Let's Meet Taylor and Melanie

One hot July evening, with the sounds of summer storms softly rumbling outside, in a small apartment, I sat down with two good friends and fellow church members from Limitless Church in Tampa, Melanie and Taylor. Melanie and Taylor, mother and son, live a life they call "their normal." "Their normal" is not the average normal. "Their normal" is truly inspiring. Melanie and Taylor have been given a very special gift from God—the gift of encouragement. Their story begins twenty four years ago on July 12th, 1995. Taylor entered this world like any other normal baby, filling mom's heart with dreams of the wonderful life ahead.

Melanie and Taylor shared their story earnestly over the rhythmic sounds of the respirator attached to Taylor's power chair, only stopping when one of their two cats injected themselves into our conversation, seeking some attention. When Taylor was just a year old, Melanie took him to the doctor because he wasn't feeling well. They performed (what she thought) were routine blood tests. They went home to await the results. The day before Thanksgiving 1996, they got a diagnosis that would change everything. Taylor was diagnosed with Duchenne Muscular Dystrophy, a progressive disease that would rob him of the use of his muscles as he got older. Melanie remembered the doctors were reluctant to give her the results of the tests they performed, only complying after she insisted. The doctors also said that Taylor was retarded and uneducable. The second diagnosis couldn't have been more wrong. Taylor not only completed high school, but graduated with honors. Melanie had not yet accepted Christ as her Lord and savior, which she said made this news all the more terrifying. Having no other outlet for her feelings, Melanie wrote a poem:

I have seen the sun rise in your eyes
And in them I will see it set.
Your spring is passing
In days when others have months.
Summer is coming.
In the fall you will fall.
I will pick you up,
But you will fall again.
Winter will be upon us.
Night will close your eyes.
And I will fall.

Taylor's early years were not easy even though he could walk on his own. He had to take steroids and other medications that made him cranky and downright unhappy. Taylor has always been quite a talker, and despite the medications, did have a very bright side. As a young boy, Taylor loved meeting pregnant women, placing his hands on their bellies and talking to the babies inside. This would always bring smiles to expectant moms. Taylor's dad passed away when Taylor was only five years old, leaving Melanie a single mom to raise two small children, one with disabilities. Taylor had appointments with doctors and speech therapists and physical therapists, among others. Melanie was Taylor's driver all the while continuing to work and support the family.

While living in Illinois, Melanie met a colonel in the Air Force who would bug her regularly to attend his church. Finally one day, she decided to go and was introduced to God. While attending the church in Illinois, Melanie would regularly write letters to God. Having never learned about prayer, the letters were her way of talking to God. Melanie soon felt very at home in the church, and the pastor there encouraged her letter writing campaign to God. He had a good sense of family; Taylor and his younger brother, Spencer, were welcomed warmly as well each and every Sunday morning.

In 2001, Melanie, Taylor, and Spencer packed up their belongings and moved to Tampa, Florida. At this time, Taylor could still walk on his own. Melanie found a new home at a church called The Crossing Church after moving to the Tampa Bay area. The pastor and church members openly accepted the small family. Due to the nature of Taylor's physical disabilities, Taylor had to change schools in second grade. As Taylor had become the heart of his class, his classmates and teachers at his first school missed him terribly. Taylor, however, thrived at his new school and it didn't take long before Taylor's charming personality won over his newfound classmates and teachers. Despite the progressive disease, Melanie made sure her boys' childhoods were as normal as possible. Taylor even served on the fifth grade Safety Patrol, a position that gave Taylor a sense of authority. He was losing authority over his body due to his disease and this newly directed authority suited him well as he used humor to express it among his classmates.

It was at The Crossing Church where Melanie was baptized. She said it was like the story from Acts 8 in the Bible where Philip encountered an Ethiopian eunuch in the desert. Like the eunuch, Melanie heard the Gospel, saw the water, and instantly wanted to proclaim Jesus Christ as her savior. There was a baptizing pool at the church, and Melanie was ready to jump right in and be baptized. She said the whole experience of being renewed in Christ was such a relief.

When Taylor was eight years old, the Make-A-Wish Foundation sent him and his family to Hawaii. It was a wonderful family vacation that left Taylor, Spencer, and Mom with great memories. It was in Hawaii where a picture of Taylor standing on a volcanic boulder was taken. That was the last picture of Taylor ever taken standing under his own strength. Taylor would soon be required to use a wheelchair as his source of mobility. For Taylor, being in a wheelchair was more freeing than confining. By that point in his life, he could hardly stand and could barely walk.

When Taylor entered high school, he began to develop a very special gift—a gift that makes me and everyone in proximity to Taylor smile. Taylor started telling jokes. He would tell jokes to anyone who would listen. Taylor even joined the football team as the equipment manager and Inspirational Team Captain. Taylor became the heart of his high school by bringing everyone together. It didn't matter if the jocks, goths, nerds, loners were in the same room; if Taylor was there, everyone knew they would be accepted, so they all got along and got to know each other a little. They would just talk and have a great time. It is no wonder Taylor made so many friends at school. Taylor had become such a celebrity at school that the local news station honored him with the title "Athlete of the Week" at his last football game as a senior. Even though his disability kept him from playing the game, he was no less a part of the team. There is even one teammate who has Taylor's name tattooed on his arm with an anchor (because Taylor helps him anchor his emotions) and wings (because Taylor is an angel).

Taylor is a magnet for all people. The light of God shines through him. Taylor will tell you that he is not the chair, "It is just how I have to get around." Taylor is not shy. He can approach anyone and is always eager to share one of his newest jokes. His favorite joke is: "*What do you get when there are too many aliens around? Extraterrestrials.*" Taylor is even writing a fictional story about aliens. I can't wait to read it. Melanie likes to remind Taylor that he is perfectly suited for the purpose God made him for. That purpose is to inspire others and make everyone smile. I will have to agree with his mom. Taylor is very good at both.

Taylor admits that he is not free from fear and anxiety. When he finally lost the use of his arms and hands, his mother had to help feed him. He didn't want to go out and eat at restaurants because he thought people would stare. Of course, no one did. When the muscles that control his breathing were just not strong enough anymore, doctors performed a tracheostomy and installed a breathing tube to be attached to a mechanical respirator to help him breathe. He thought people would stare and he was uncomfortable going out in public again. Taylor has such a charismatic personality that I don't think people even notice he is in a chair, let alone his breathing tube. It is so easy to look right past all the devices that assist him with his disability and just see Taylor—a vibrant young man with a heart the size of Texas.

Melanie shared a vision she had with me. She prefaced it by explaining that she had prayed to God to give her the vision of Taylor entering heaven. She wanted to see it before Taylor passes as something she might find comfort in. God answered her prayer and allowed her to see it. Melanie said, "There was a narrow stone archway at the entrance of a long tunnel. From the other end of the tunnel, an unimaginably bright light illuminated the passageway." She went on to say, "Taylor walked through the archway and into the tunnel. After walking a ways in, he turned to her and with a giant grin, he began to dance and wave his arms all the way into heaven." Melanie had such a big smile on her face as she shared her vision of Taylor dancing into heaven. It is a vision that gives her great comfort.

Taylor worries from time to time about dying. He says since he does bad things every now and again, he gets uncomfortable with the idea of not getting into heaven. His mother always tells him that as long as he believes in Jesus, he will be okay. That usually makes him feel better, he said.

Melanie and Taylor found their way to Limitless Church in Tampa through the high school Taylor attended. There was a mobile church that used to meet there on Sunday mornings. Pastor Matt Blair would always support the high school's events by attending football games and volunteering all of the church members to help out where the school needed it. So when Taylor needed a risky surgery to fuse his entire spine, Melanie reached out to the church she attended with Taylor and got no response. Pastor Matt Blair heeded God's command to randomly call people who had been to church at exactly the time Melanie needed to know God was there. He rallied the troops to pray for and support Taylor through his surgery. Matt even visited Taylor in the hospital. After Taylor's discharge from the hospital and recovery, the two were hooked on Limitless Church and have attended ever since.

One of the scarier moments with his condition happened a year or so ago. Taylor was suffering from three different infections all at one time. Taylor's first symptom was losing his sight completely for a little more than fifteen minutes and turning gray, the color of old oatmeal. Melanie called 911 and Taylor was raced to the emergency room. By the time he got to the ER, he had regained his sight and was treated for the infections. In the ER that day, Taylor's bright, inspiring outlook on life charmed the ER staff and the emergency responders that got him there. Taylor is a constant light that brightens everyone's day even when his disease is challenging him. Taylor credits God's love for his gift to be able to do that.

Taylor has a prayer for someone in need every night before bed. He is always thinking of others. Despite his disabling condition, Taylor puts all his trust in God's love, and in so doing, he reflects that love on to those around him. Taylor and Melanie are two of the most inspiring people I have ever met. Melanie has dedicated her life to making sure Taylor is well taken care of. She will tell you that God chose her to be Taylor's mom.

Both Taylor and Melanie, given the hand they have been dealt, could easily turn their backs on God. They could be angry at the world. They could handle this situation with a bleak, sad outlook on life. They, however, choose to love God and place their faith in Christ. This has given them strength beyond what an average person could muster. Taylor knows deep in his heart that he has a purpose. He knows that God's love for him is the reason behind his purpose. Taylor told me he loves how the equation $F = TL^3$ illustrates so simply his faith and purpose here on earth.

The life expectancy for someone with Duchenne Muscular Dystrophy is from mid to late twenties. Taylor and Melanie will tell you with confidence that he is going to make it to his forties. During the process of editing and formatting this book Taylor died twice. The first time Taylor died, the battery in his respirator ran out of power. Taylor's brother Spencer found him unconscious without a pulse. Spencer started CPR and was able to get Taylor's heart beating by the time First Responders arrived. Spencer had saved his brother's life. Taylor spent the next two days in a coma. The doctors had no idea of the extent Taylor would recover from his accident. Prayers immediately started to pour in from around the world and Taylor regained consciousness seemingly no worse for the incident. Over the next few days Taylor developed a few complications with his breathing equipment. Taylor's heart stopped a second time. Doctors spent twenty minutes performing chest compressions that would break all of Taylor's ribs. The Sisterhood group from Limitless Church raced to the hospital and began prayer and worship. More prayers poured in and Taylor came through a second time. Taylor is back home telling jokes and shining his light on all who meet him. Prayer was integral in helping Taylor through his experience. God does amazing things through prayer. I regularly pray for Taylor and his mom and am truly blessed to know them both.

Let's Meet Scott

I met Scott four years ago while serving at Limitless Church in Tampa, Florida on a hot, sunny Sunday morning. My son and I had started helping with set up in the Children's Ministry area. Since we were a mobile church meeting at a local high school, this required us to move classroom tables and chairs then lay out rubber mats that fit together like a puzzle to prepare for the children attending each Sunday morning. Scott showed up that morning eager to help. Jim, one of the other church members in charge of setup, had Scott put out signs and pull-up shades which required a little coordination. Scott, having suffered a stroke several years earlier, thought it would be a worthy challenge and perhaps therapeutic at the same time so he happily accepted his assignment. The Sunday morning setup team of about six guys would, after completion, meet at a local McDonald's for breakfast before church services started for some fellowship time.

Scott's story doesn't start here though. Scott grew up in Maryland with his two older brothers. As kids, their mom would take them to church regularly until Scott was about seven or eight years old. Dad wasn't much of a churchgoer and didn't show signs of supporting their regular Sunday morning ritual. As a result, the three boys slowly lost interest in church and Mom stopped taking them. When Scott was thirteen, his parents divorced. Mom remarried when Scott was around sixteen. The new step dad was a deeply religious man and drew Mom back to church. The brothers were just a little too old to be influenced into reattending church.

Scott soon graduated high school and went off to college. After a rocky freshman year at the university, Scott turned things around, improved his grades, and became an academic advisor after graduating. Scott credits the poor academic performance during his freshman year to giving him the insight to help young students entering the college scene as an advisor. He was able to give advice from personal experience. During this period of Scott's life, he did believe in something greater than himself in a spiritual way. He believed his deceased grandfather was looking out for him and he would often talk to his grandfather, which to him felt like prayer. Scott says it was his early experience attending church that left his spiritual window open even if it wasn't God whom he was praying to.

Scott moved to Colorado at the age of thirty and moved into his brother's apartment. Scott and his brother enjoyed the single life in Denver for several years. It was in these years that Scott started dating a young woman who was a former Mormon. She left her Mormon roots but did continue to follow a faith in Christ. She soon had Scott attending church again. Scott had been looking for fulfillment. He felt as though he was missing something and attending church started to fill that void in his life. The relationship later ended and Scott found himself doing other things on Sunday morning rather than attending church.

At thirty-five, Scott decided to move out of his brother's house and get a place of his own. Scott soon started seeing a married woman who was going through a divorce, which proved to be somewhat toxic. He was working a job he didn't like and started to feel very empty once more. At thirty-nine, Scott suffered from a bad case of strep throat and the doctors told him he should watch his blood pressure as it was quite high. Like most guys, the doctor's warnings went to the back of the mind and eventually forgotten altogether. After several years in a rut, Scott got a job working in the mortgage industry as a division manager and was traveling through several states. Scott's brother was also working at the same company and had made quite a name for himself. Everything, however, was going to change for Scott.

Two days before Scott's fortieth birthday, his brother was planning a surprise party for him. Scott doesn't particularly like surprises so all his friends were, of course, happy to make him feel uncomfortable with the party. It was a "guy thing," Scott says. That day, Scott was feeling a little off. It was Veteran's Day so Scott was at home. His left side was numb and he felt unsteady, so he called his brother. After explaining some symptoms to his brother, his brother told him to hang up and he would call back shortly. Within a matter of minutes, there was a team of emergency responders buzzing in at the front door of his condo building. The EMTs performed several tests and then rushed Scott to the hospital just down the road. When Scott's brother called all their friends to cancel the surprise party due to Scott having a stroke, they all thought it was a joke because Scott didn't like surprises. Scott's brother had to tell them a second time that he had a real stroke.

At the hospital, Scott was diagnosed with having suffered a hemorrhagic stroke, which is a full bleed on the brain. The stroke was on the right side of his brain and affected the use of the left side of his body. Scott was sedated to assist in the healing process and as a result has no memory from Thursday afternoon to Tuesday the following week. Scott said he was so out of it that he tried to use the TV remote to call his girlfriend at the time.

When Scott regained his consciousness, he learned that the stroke rendered the left side of his body immobile. He couldn't walk or use his left hand. His speech was affected as well and his lip drooped on the left side of his face. He did, however, woke to the faces of his loving and supportive family. The next day, Scott was transported to the University of Colorado Hospital where he stayed for a full month while being treated for the stroke. He went through occupational, physical, and speech therapy while in the hospital. He said it would take him forty-five minutes to walk around the one floor of the hospital during his month-long recovery. Scott even had the family Thanksgiving feast right there in the hospital.

Scott was discharged from the hospital in mid-December and he found himself living back with his brother. Scott was determined to get back to being self-sufficient and would move back into his own home in May of the next year. When Scott and his brother went to the airport to pick up their mom, Scott stubbornly left his cane in the car, forcing himself to walk through Denver Airport. It was quite a challenge but Scott powered through it and did it. Mom was not happy with the decision but that didn't deter Scott. Scott's mom would help him along in his recovery by working through word problems with him to regain some of the lost mental acuity. He would do laps around his brother's house to improve his walking. It was precisely sixty-five steps and he would count each step through the arduous journey. He was also given a machine that would assist him with regaining strength in his left hand. His therapist would continue to work with him for a full three years.

Scott had only been working for his current employer for four months when he had his stroke. The company was so understanding that they assured him his job would be waiting for him when he returned. It took four months of recovery before he was ready to go back to work. Upon returning to work, he started up his rigorous travel schedule which proved to be exhausting. The effects of the stroke were making it difficult for Scott to continue on in his role. After two years of tiring travel, Scott asked if there was another position at the company he could take on. His boss said they were building a reporting division and that he would be perfect for the job.

Recovering from a stroke is an ongoing process and Scott found therapy in walking. The Denver winters are cold and the high altitude took its toll on Scott due to the aftereffects of his stroke. So in 2015, Scott asked his boss if he could move to Florida where the weather is always warm and more conducive to his walking therapy. His boss approved the move. His family was apprehensive about him moving to Florida but Scott was determined. It was at this time that Scott felt God moving through him. Scott sold his house ten minutes after listing it in Denver and found a home two days later in the Tampa area. "That was God letting me know the move to Florida was the best for me," Scott said.

Scott's mom and step dad were strong in faith and encouraged Scott to seek out a church in his new town. They felt it would help him in the transition and he could get the help he needed from a strong church family. Scott's new neighbor was attending a new church plant in the area and invited Scott to attend as well. Scott came to Limitless Church the very next Sunday where he met Pastor Matt Blair. Pastor Matt encouraged Scott to come to Sunday morning setup and serve on the team. This brings me to the day I met Scott as we read in the first paragraph.

The church has since moved to a new school location for Sunday services and the setup team meets on Friday evenings to get the church ready for Sunday service, but Scott, my son, and I still meet every Sunday morning for breakfast before church. We have had to tone down some of the sophomoric banter as my daughter joins us occasionally. Scott has become one of my closest friends and I have had the honor of watching Scott grow in his faith over the past four years. Scott told me that he now prays to Jesus but still says hi to his grandfather. Scott credits his continued recovery to his newly found faith in God's love. Scott, too, loves the simple yet profound expression of the equation $F = TL^3$. He proudly wears the T-shirts we had printed up sporting the equation on the front.

Like the others who have shared their stories in this book, Scott could have walked a path of anger and self-pity as a result of having his stroke and being left with a limp and little use of his hand. He chose not to, though. Scott chose to seek out the love of God and all the strength that comes with that love. Scott still struggles with daily life, but the love God has poured into those around him at church continues to flow into him. Scott will tell you he has never felt so at home as he does at Limitless. Scott also says one of the biggest turning points was when he got involved in the small groups offered at Limitless. Scott's faith continues to grow and I look forward to being a witness to his journey. Scott is truly a great friend and inspiration.

Let's Meet Pastor Erin Blair

Erin is the wife of Pastor Matt Blair and together, they planted Limitless Church in Tampa, Florida. Erin's story isn't one you would expect from a beautiful upper middle-class family that poured an endless supply of love into each other. Her story, however, is becoming more and more prevalent in today's society.

"Free." Free is the word Erin used to describe how she felt the first time she smoked pot and drank alcohol at the young age of twelve. She said she felt free from all the anxiety and depression that plagued her young mind. She thought she was finally free from the pressure and pain boiling up inside her. Erin believed she had found the answer to it all. All she found, however, was the door that would let Satan in and allow his attacks to torture her and her family for years to come. Erin explains that addiction doesn't just happen. It slithers its way into someone's life and slowly begins to choke out the light until all that is seen is darkness. All hopes, dreams, and aspirations fade into a well of extreme darkness. Life becomes a battle of survival by feeding the dark within.

Erin grew up in a home that showered love over her. She was aware of just how much her family loved her. It was her battle with clinical anxiety and depression that led to a tremendous feeling of emptiness on the inside that she didn't know how to express. After all, how could she?

She was only twelve years old. When the emptiness appeared to be filled through drugs and alcohol, she began to pursue these chemical masks as a way to numb her pain.

At the age of fifteen, Erin began dating a boy whom her parents would not approve of, so she kept it a secret from them. The secret she had to keep led to lies as well and she found this to be very painful, as she knew the pain it would cause them for they loved her dearly. When Erin learned of her boyfriend cheating on her, she was devastated. She felt she could no longer go on living. She swallowed a handful of pills and washed them down with the liquor from her parents' cabinet. In that moment, she was trying to escape the unbearable pain. A friend of Erin's came over when she started having a seizure. Erin was rushed to the emergency room where doctors and nurses pumped her stomach. Her father was there holding her hand tightly as tears welled up in his eyes. Erin was so full of shame and embarrassment that she couldn't look at her father. When asked why she took the pills and alcohol, she replied, "I just wanted to sleep for a very long time."

Erin was then admitted to a mental institution. Erin was greeted by a boy she had gone to high school with but she didn't recognize him. His haunting words stay with her to this day: "Who would have thought that someone like you would end in a place like this with people like us?" You see, Erin portrayed a person that had it all together. She was a cheerleader, honor roll student, member of the homecoming court and student council. On the inside, however, she was falling apart. The doctors there diagnosed her with clinical depression and started her on a treatment plan that could be best described as a long search for finding the right concoction of medicines that could bring Erin some relief.

After being discharged, Erin found herself skipping school to go home and sleep off the effects of her new meds. The medicine left her very sleepy and lethargic. Erin had to forge notes from her parents excusing her abundant absences from school. This, of course, led her to getting into a lot of trouble with the school and threatened her ability to graduate that year. Erin had already been accepted to the University of North Carolina at Wilmington and she needed to graduate to go on to college. Erin's mom helped her meet with school officials and with Mom's loving guidance, Erin was cleared to graduate on time.

One week prior to graduation, Erin's parents told her that she and the family were going to go to Minneapolis for a convention her father had to attend for work. That was just a cover to get Erin to eagerly accompany the family to Minnesota. When they arrived, they pulled up to Hazelden Rehab Center; Erin knew there was no convention and began screaming and crying. Erin's father produced a letter from the Department of Motor Vehicles stating that she had to complete twenty-eight days of rehab followed by living in a halfway house for several months to get her driver's license reinstated. Several weeks prior, Erin received a DUI and this was her sentence for the offense. While all of Erin's friends walked across the graduation stage, Erin would spend her graduation day in a rehab center hundreds of miles from home.

Erin's stay at the rehab center would only last a week. Erin broke the rules and disobeyed in an attempt to get kicked out. She did realize while there that her relationship with her boyfriend was abusive and unhealthy, but she never thought she had a problem with drugs and alcohol. After her first week, Erin was taken to a Greyhound bus station for the thirty-six-hour trip from Minneapolis to Greensboro. Halfway back to North Carolina, at around 1:00 a.m., Erin was dropped off at a bus station in the middle of nowhere. She was terrified. God was with her that night. With her at the station was a couple, a pastor and his wife. The two comforted her until she left for home.

Back in Greensboro, Erin's mom set boundaries. Mom had been educating herself about addiction and sought counseling as well. Erin was distanced from the family to protect her brother from her dysfunctional behavior. Her friends had all gone off to college and she had no driver's license to go visit them. Erin started experimenting with more drugs and continued her abusive relationship with her boyfriend. This was when Erin started praying for the first time. Erin was praying for a way out. A way out of the circumstances she created for herself. Erin was too weak to break free on her own and she knew only through God could she find the strength to lift herself out. The young man she was seeing at the time was sentenced to four years in prison, and slowly, she started to see the world around her. She saw those hurting around her, something she had never noticed before. Life to this point revolved around Erin. She never looked up to see those around her. But now, somehow, she was awakened. After visiting her boyfriend in prison for about a year, she came to the realization she wanted to help all those people who were hurting in the world. She wanted to help the people she once judged negatively. God planted a purpose in Erin's heart, but God still had some refining to do. Erin knew she was not yet ready to help others as she hadn't yet helped herself.

Erin attended college the following summer with her parents' help. She joined a sorority and ended her abusive relationship. Erin had yet to help herself heal and spent the next three years in college using cocaine, ecstasy, and alcohol to blur reality. She found herself sleeping with multiple partners and was almost raped while passed out one night. Erin bounced around from one abusive relationship to another and lost a child in early pregnancy due to her cocaine use. She even received a second DUI. Erin would regularly lay on the bathroom floor in fetal position, pulling out her hair and screaming in an attempt to find an escape. Erin's plan was not going well. Erin contemplated suicide every day for over two years and fell into trouble with the law. Erin knew something had to give.

On February 21, 2002, Erin checked herself into a drug and alcohol rehab center with one prayer on her heart: "God, who I am going in is *not* who I want to be when I get out!" Erin walked through those doors, took off her mask, and laid herself out before God. She submitted all authority to the Father. It would be through her total trust in God's love that she would gather the strength to allow Jesus to fully transform her.

Rehab was not easy. Erin had to deal with years of painful emotions, fear, anxiety, and doubt. She would have to place it all on God. God's steadfast, limitless love was all she had left in this world. When the triggers that would stir up her temptations came upon her, she would find relief through her encounters with God. As it states in **Psalm 34:8 ESV, "Oh, taste and see**

that the Lord is good!" Erin would experience this through her prayers. Through the "tasting," Erin was given just enough light through the darkness to take the next courageous step on her path to recovery.

Erin would regularly recommit herself to Jesus, and through prayer, ask for life and the ability to help and inspire others who battle with addiction. In rehab, Erin learned that the enemy comes to kill, steal, and destroy. It was just the beginning of a radical transformation as Erin began to walk out of the pit of hell that had engulfed her for years and overtaken her body, soul, and spirit. Jesus truly rescued her and took her to higher ground where the chains were broken and she was *free* to live a life without addiction. Erin used the passion and fire she was born with. Rather than using it for the world as she had for years, she used it for Christ! **Genesis 50:20 ESV** (emphasis mine), **"As for you, you [Satan] meant evil against me but God meant it for good."** What was once fueling Erin's addiction began to fuel her faith. Erin says she was healed that year. God healed her in just one year, yet without him, it would have taken a lifetime.

Following rehab, Erin went back to school and studied psychology and wanted to become a substance abuse counselor. She wanted to help others find the freedom she ultimately found. She immersed herself in the Body of Christ, associating with others on a similar faith journey. Six months into her sobriety, she began attending a college ministry each and every week. It was through the Body of Christ that she found people willing to accept her and get down deep into the trenches with her to help her become whom God had planned for her to be.

Erin was introduced to a worship leader in the college ministry. He had an amazing voice that brought Erin to the feet of Jesus every time he sang. Over time, Erin opened up to the worship leader and spoke to him of her past. Erin feared that he would run away knowing who she once was, but it seemed to draw him closer to her. Erin had never been treated with such respect and gentleness as this man had treated her. He would open doors for Erin, which was a new experience for her. She joked with him saying, "Wow, what are you going to do next? Roll out a red carpet?" Sure enough, the next time he picked her up for the ministry meetings, he rolled out a red carpet for her. This brave and gentle man was Matt Blair. Erin made a commitment not to date during her first year of sobriety as men were as much of a drug as cocaine or alcohol. Matt patiently waited out her first year and was just a good friend to Erin. After that first year ended, Matt and Erin started dating. They eventually got engaged and married. They now have four beautiful daughters and recently adopted their son.

Erin says, "Had I written out dreams for what I wanted my life to look like, it wouldn't come close to this! The radical transformation I have experienced has given me a heart for hurting people. I started a nonprofit, Five14 Revolution, to raise awareness about human trafficking by reaching out to women in strip clubs. The strip club I used to party in while living through the darkest of times is one I was able to deliver a message of hope by living in the light. The treatment facility I entered fourteen years ago hired me to work for them after being sober for six months. I worked checking in patients, talking with family members, and leading group time. Eventually, my mom helped open a treatment facility in Kentucky where there is a room called Erin's Miracle. My story is printed on the wall. I have been able to meet with the women there and encourage them! Learning how to be healthy in my body, soul, and spirit was a journey I embarked on when getting clean. That has led me to be in various roles over the years from being a health/fitness coach to life coach. I am now overseeing our women's ministry at the church my husband Matt and I planted in Tampa called Limitless Sisterhood!" Helping people find freedom is her heart's cry and life's purpose.

The word "freedom" is a banner over Erin's life. Erin allowed Jesus' story to become her story. Erin spent years pursuing sex, drugs, and alcohol in an attempt to fill the void in her life, but it was her trusting in Jesus that filled it. She was looking for Jesus all along. All she had to do was look up and trust. Erin told me the following: "If ever there is a time to get free, it is now! God needs us in this world to be hope. He needs us for furthering his message of forgiveness through the cross and an abundant life through his resurrection. The power that raised him is the power within us! We are made to overcome! We are made to conquer! We are made to rise above! We're not defeated, weak-minded victims in the world. We have a story to tell and a voice to shout it. The only way to break free is to know Jesus more every day. He will give you your purpose but you have to stay the course. You have to prune some bushes here and there and cut off those who are not helping you become whom God has created you to be. You have to guard your heart against offense and bitterness. You have to be willing to be uncomfortable in order to experience more of God. This is abundant living and it is available for all! Give your pain to Jesus, and in return, he'll give you purpose and you will become unstoppable and live the limitless life you were born for!" Erin found her freedom through placing all her trust in the love of God.

"The LORD is my light and my salvation; whom shall I fear?"
(Psalm 27:1 ESV)

"For I am the LORD your God who takes hold of your right hand and says to you, Do not fear; I will help you."
(Isaiah 41:13 NIV)

Each of the testimonies we have read represents extreme adversity. The enemy was at full war with each of these individuals. They all found a strength through the love of God to overcome the very difficult times they encountered. They knew Jesus was there supporting them through very difficult times. As I interviewed each of these good friends, I shared with them the equation $F = TL^3$. When I asked them what they thought of the equation, each and every time, they each said "yes," that equation illustrates the source of the strength they received to overcome what seemed like insurmountable obstacles. They each placed so much trust in the love of God that even terrifying, life-threatening troubles were uprooted, turned over, and defeated by God. They each understood and placed trust in the unending, steadfast love of God.

CHAPTER 6

WHAT NEXT?

W e have learned how to apply the equation $F = TL^3$ to our daily prayer time and our daily lives as Christians. We have heard the testimonies of real people who have been impacted by the triune love of God and what it means to them to place all their trust in that love. So, what is next?

What is next? The two Sundays following Easter 2019, Pastor Matt Blair of Limitless Church in Tampa, Florida, in preparation of baptisms after service, preached on this very topic. The topic of "what is next?" As Pastor Matt prepared for baptisms, he was inspired to help those being baptized that day as well as the rest of the congregation to understand the next step. What should we do after we make a public proclamation of our accepting Jesus Christ as our Lord and savior? Pastor Matt said, "Tell someone! Share the joy you are experiencing in this moment so that others can see your example and be drawn to Christ as well." This is the next step for the equation $F = TL^3$ also.

This simple and beautiful expression of our faith, $F = TL^3$, has become a beacon, a light that reminds me each day of the full extent of God's love for all of us. It reminds me of the sacrifice God made, the bloodshed, the true cost of our salvation. In reminding us of this, we can pray over this equation to help pull us through difficult times. To know God will always be there for us. He will never leave our side. This equation can bring us back from being self-absorbed with success to keeping a right relationship with God by thanking, praising, and worshiping him for our provision. Yes! The next step is to tell someone. Share the equation. Use it to start a conversation. If we have a tool that can so concisely express all the joy God's love gives us, why would we not share it? I can think of nothing more selfish, nothing that would please Satan more than keeping this a secret. Please don't keep it a secret.

Bill Cates, a professional sales coach, public speaker, and best-selling author, wrote a book on the subject of getting referrals. Obtaining referrals is something that most sales people struggle with. Bill was my sales coach back in the early 1990s, so when his book was published, I was eager to read it. The title of this book was *Please Don't Keep Me a Secret*. I know God doesn't want to be kept a secret. God wants us to share our experiences as Christians and reflect his love out onto the world. Bill's catch phrase, "Don't keep me a secret," is very fitting for this equation and for God as well. Let's tell everyone we see about the love God pours into us each and every day. Let's share this equation with anyone who will listen.

Share with others the impact of what placing trust in God's love has had on your faith and life. If it has helped you through a difficult time, share it. If it has simply helped you focus on and grow in your relationship with Jesus, share it. If it has helped you have a conversation with someone that you may not have otherwise had a conversation with, share it. If it has brought you closer to your spouse, children, family, and friends, share it. The message is far too important to keep a secret. Share it!

"Therefore go and make disciples of all nations, baptizing them in the name of the Father and of the Son and of the Holy Spirit..."

(Matthew 28:19 NIV)

Now that we have an understanding how this equation can be used as a tool in our daily Christian lives, let's discuss how we might use it as a tool to disciple others. As the next several chapters will discuss, nonbelievers often substitute some other idolatrous term for the triune love of God, L^3. Nonbelievers place their trust in something other than truth, such as worldly things like money, power, self, job, beauty, fame, sex, drugs and alcohol, and many other things that seem to give them satisfaction at the moment. These will only provide fleeting relief. Nothing listed here is rooted in truth and therefore cannot provide a firm foundation for faith or life.

The following chapters will show you how substituting God's love with any other term will break down and fail. The following examples will show the reader how, in a simple conversation, to run through this equation using substitutions. These substitutions will cause everything to break down and lead a person down a path of uncertainty, anxiety, fear, loneliness, and ultimately, death. It is detrimental to build a foundation of faith on these temporary worldly things.

"No one can serve two masters. Either he will hate the one and love the other, or you will be devoted to one and despise the other. You cannot serve both God and money."

(MATTHEW 6:24 NIV)

"He who loves money will not be satisfied with money, nor he who loves wealth with his income; this also is vanity."

(ECCLESIASTES 5:10 ESV)

$F = T\$^6$. Let's explore replacing L^3 the triune love of God, with the term $\$^6$—representing money or more precisely, the "dollar to the power of six." Why "$" to the power of "6"? Because there are six zeroes in a million. Everyone who dreams of being rich typically dreams of being a millionaire. This equation represents living a life that puts the love of money first, front and center, before God and others. If our faith is based on our trust in or love of money, a temporary, finite, ever-changing, corruptible, materialistic term, then the product—our faith—will be temporary, finite, ever-changing, and corruptible as well. Faith, in this, case won't be the rock solid foundation on which to build principles.

I do want to be clear. I am not condemning money, the need for money, or any currency for that matter. We live in a God-created society that operates with a God-created economy. Money is not bad. Money is, in fact, a necessity. Jesus speaks about money all through the New Testament. He tells the parable of the wealthy man that entrusts his servants with his wealth—one with five bags of gold, one with three bags, and one with one bag—in Matthew 25:14–30. Daniel is portrayed as a good and trustworthy steward of the king's wealth in the Book of Daniel. Money has always had a place in society. It is, however, important to be sure the order of importance money plays in our lives is appropriately positioned. That we don't allow our love for money to overshadow our love for God.

Saving is important as well. **"On the first day of every week, each one of you should set aside a sum of money in keeping with your income, saving it up, so that when I come no collections will have to be made" (1 Corinthians 16:2 NIV).** Being a good steward with what God provides is important to God. The problem comes from greed. When we put our love and trust in money before trust and love for God and our neighbors, we are on unstable ground. Those who seek wealth at the expense of others and at the expense of God fall far short of God's will for them.

We learned in the first few chapters that God's love is true, constant, infinite, limitless, and unwavering. The dollar has none of these characteristics. The dollar is not constant. The dollar is finite, temporary, and volatile. The value of the dollar fluctuates daily on the currency exchanges. Over time, inflation devalues the dollar. In 1967, the average price of a new car was $2,750, the average monthly rent was $125 per month, and gas was thirty-three cents per gallon. In 2019, the average price for a new car is $36,590, the average monthly rent is $1,430 per month, and gas is $3 per gallon. The average price of these items has increased approximately ten times in the last fifty-two years. That means a person has to pay ten times more for those things today than they did the year I was born.

The amount of money in your bank account fluctuates as well. You earn money at work so money is deposited in your account. You have to pay bills so money is removed from your account. Unexpected costs for things such as auto repairs, appliance repairs, and medical expenses can and will erode the amount of money in your accounts even faster. If we lose our job, we lose our ability to acquire money while unemployed. Money is anything but constant.

The dollar is tied to the US economy and now, more than ever, it is tied to many of the world's economies. These economies can be volatile. Economic downturns devalue the dollar. Investments are also very volatile. The performance of investment portfolios is tied to world economies as well. Stock prices are based on a number of factors. One of those factors is a company's earnings. Companies are run by people. People are imperfect and prone to making mistakes. People are subject to emotions like greed. People are capable of lying, cheating, and fraud. The unwary investor can be blindsided by these evils. Take cases like WorldCom in the early 2000s. Bernard Ebbers overstated cash flows of WorldCom which resulted in an estimated $100 billion loss. Enron's Kenneth Lay and Jeffrey Skilling falsified financial results causing $74 billion in losses, much of which was in Enron employees' retirement accounts, rendering those accounts worthless. Bernie Madoff lost investors an estimated $65 billion in a pyramid scheme. There have been thousands of cases like these in the past and there will be thousands of cases like these in years to come. Money is a product of this earthly world and is subject to being manipulated for evil and, therefore, is corruptible.

When we place all our trust in finite, temporary things, we can be driven to worry, anxiety, fear, and uncertainty. I know this firsthand. From 1994 to 2006, I was a stock broker. I was driven to make as much money as I could. I wanted the fancy cars, the big house, and everything that came with wealth. On the surface, this was not a bad thing. There is nothing wrong with wanting to be wealthy. There is nothing wrong with wanting nice things. My problem was, that was all I was. I identified myself with the money I made and invested. Money was what I was building my principles on. This was a very unstable place to be.

I regularly woke in the middle of the night with panic attacks, worrying about how I was going to make it through the next month. I found myself lying about who I was and what I was worth to try and gain the trust of investors. "Fake it till you make it" was the motto many of the advisors I used to work with as we tried to build our careers. This led to a feeling of doubt and being unfulfilled. Over the years, I made a lot of money yet never felt fulfilled. I always wanted more. I never felt like I could just be friends with people. I always tried to find just the right angle to make them my client. Everything revolved around making more money. I was placing money in this equation where God's love should have been. As a result of also being an atheist in those years, I didn't even know what constant term I should have placed in the equation. I did not yet understand that I was building a life on a very unstable foundation. A foundation of principles that would eventually lead me to leaving the investment business and starting a new career from scratch. I did, however, after twelve years as a financial advisor, realize that being a financial advisor was not the profession God had planned for me to spend a lifetime doing. God ultimately had different plans for me. It would take God another thirteen years to refine me into the person he had planned for me to be.

By no means am I condemning the profession of a financial advisor. God has placed this noble profession on the hearts of many good, capable people, most of which are honest and trustworthy. In fact, I still have many friends in the industry whom I would trust managing my own money.

As a financial advisor, I had two clients in the late 1990s—a young man and his mother. Both he and his mother hired me to manage their money around 1996 and each invested $100,000. By the end of 1999, both accounts were each worth over $300,000. The accounts tripled in three years and I was feeling pretty good about myself. In November of 1999, the son called me to let me know he and his mother were firing me as they thought the accounts should have grown to over one million dollars each. He accused me of being too conservative and told me he could do a better job himself. Several months later on March 10, 2000, the tech bubble burst. Approximately four months after that, the son called me and asked if we could meet as soon as possible, it was urgent. I agreed and met him at his mother's house.

When I arrived there was a "for sale" sign on the front lawn, the house was empty of all the furniture, and my former client was lying on the floor in the fetal position sobbing. When I asked him what was wrong, he said he had lost everything including his mother's home. He had invested all the money including a second mortgage on his mother's home in just two companies. Both companies lost 95% of their value in a few short weeks. He said he wanted me to help him earn it all back, but he had nothing. I felt a deep pity for this young man. I was unable to help him.

I learned a week later that my former client committed suicide. In the grip of greed and desire for money, this young man made a lot of mistakes. He lost his money and his mother's money. He was wrought with guilt, self-loathing, and tremendous anxiety over the loss of all that money and ultimately took his own life. In the equation he expressed for himself, God's love was replaced with money. My client placed all his trust in the "almighty" dollar and it led not only to his financial ruin but also his death.

This story was not unique. I read about similar stories time and time again during my years as a stock broker. Could this tragedy have been avoided? I believe it could have. As I reflect on this client's story, it clearly stands out as one of the worst. I had hundreds of clients and most of their stories fell somewhere in the middle of worst to best. So, whose story represented the best? Did I have a client that never wavered on his faith and always placed his trust in God's love first? Yes, I did.

A retired physician hired me to manage his retirement around the same time as the young man and his mother in the previous example. This gentleman was different, though. He wasn't greedy. In fact, he was very generous. A devout Christian. He regularly sent me requests to donate money to different charities and missions. During our regular talks, he would always bring up his faith and attempt to introduce me to Jesus Christ. I usually rebuked him but he never stopped trying.

Looking back on it, I should have listened. For every investment recommendation I made, he would always reply, "Give me some time to pray on that, David. I will call you back shortly." My client always called back in a timely fashion and would either agree to invest or not to invest. Even though not every investment worked out, I later realized he was my most successful client over all those years. He never lost sight of what he based his principles on. It was always God's love. He never replaced L^3 with $\$^6$. Every decision he made went through God first. As a result, he was never anxious or worried. He didn't sweat the investments that lost and didn't boast about the investments that won. He often talked me off the ledge when I was feeling anxious and uncertain about the portfolio's performance or my career. He had a very calming tone and spoke with great wisdom. I always felt so much better after speaking with him.

He would be so happy to know I finally found my way to Christ. His example was one that I often held on to as I made my way to Christ. He passed away several years ago, but his spirit in Christ stays with me always.

From these examples, we can easily see how by placing money ahead instead of God's love, our faith becomes weak because it is built on a trust in a temporary, finite, and ever shifting foundation. Money is not a constant. It is a moving target that can consume a person. $F = T\$^6$ fails to provide a product that a person can base life-giving principles in. The example of the young man who lost everything is an extreme example. It does, however, illustrate that it can lead to worry, anxiety, loss of sleep, and uncertainty. These can be overwhelming emotions that drive us even further from God. This can be a whirlpool dragging us down emotionally as well.

Not only can placing all our trust and desire in money separate us from God, it can also drive families apart and turn friends into enemies.

One of the most common reasons families fall apart is over money. I had a client who passed away around 1998. His family argued and fought over who should get what from his estate. They eventually stopped talking to one another. Unfortunately, the family did not have a will in place, so the estate ended up in probate. I don't think my client ever expected such quarrelling among his wife and kids. When I recommended he set up a will, he would always say his net worth wasn't enough to warrant it.

I was very surprised myself by how the family reacted to the distribution of Dad's wealth. I had spent many evenings at family get-togethers and they all seemed to be so happy. They all seemed to love each other very much. So what happened? They lost sight of what was important. They lost sight because they all replaced their desire for God's love with a desire for money. They were listening to a lie. The lie that money was the most import thing in their lives and would even change their lives for the better. Once the estate had settled, the son spent all his inheritance on parties and sex. The daughter spent all her inheritance on supporting her drug habit. Mom spent her money trying to bail out her children from their mistakes. In the end, they all had nothing. After witnessing the fall-out of the family feud and the subsequent squandering of the entire estate, I would say this family lost a great deal. They lost more than money. They lost their love for one another and their love for God. I lost touch with this family but I pray they turned and looked up at a loving, pursuing God and found redemption.

People will lie, cheat, and steal for money. People will even kill for it. Money can be very corruptible. There are stories in the news about robberies and murders perpetrated over money. We all know people who have lied and cheated a friend or family member over money. My ex-wife lied to authorities about me with the hopes of getting more child support money. It is a recurring theme in society. Too many people selfishly desire after money with the hope of being fulfilled. In the end, there is no fulfillment. The never-ending single-minded pursuit of money is usually just a slippery slope leading to more anxiety, worry, uncertainty, anger, feelings of unworthiness and emptiness. When we apply all our trust in money, our pursuit of money is inevitably at the expense of others. $F = T\$^6$ fails as a viable equation for faith.

One can extend the pursuit of money to the pursuit of possessions. $F = T(M_p^\$)$: Faith equals trust in material possessions to the power of money. The pursuit of money and possessions are interconnected. Acquiring possessions requires money to do so. When our faith is firmly planted in the pursuit and love of material possessions, we again lose the ability to trust that our faith has the foundational stability to develop the principles on which to base our lives. This is because all material, worldly things wear out, run down, break, get lost or stolen, and are eventually discarded.

"Want, want, want" is the motto of the person who puts material possessions first before God and others. This is an exhausting pursuit. Your life is like being on a never-ending treadmill, always trying to keep up with the newest trend and replacing the old things that run down and break.

"Take care, and be on your guard against all covetousness, for one's life does not consist in the abundance of his possessions."
(LUKE 12:15 ESV)

Everyone needs material possessions to live. Clothing, shelter, transportation, etc., are a few of life's necessities. It is when possessions become the primary focus and pursuit in one's life that materialism becomes idolatry. So many people identify themselves by the things they own. People fall into the trap of "Keeping up with the Joneses," always focused on what they don't have rather than what they do have by definition, though that is not who we are. Our relationship with Jesus Christ defines us. By putting possessions of any kind before God is very dangerous. When things are going well and we have everything we need—a good job, good income, nice cars, nice house, regular vacations—is when one can find themselves believing there is no room for God in their life. People start believing that they themselves are in control of their own destiny, but nothing could be further from the truth. That is when they are one financial mistake away from disaster, one market correction away from financial distress. This is a precarious position to be in.

"But those who desire to be rich fall into temptation, into a snare, into many senseless and harmful desires that plunge people into ruin and destruction."

(1 Timothy 6:9 ESV)

Material possessions are not constants by which to define ourselves or to build principles on which to live by. Material things are temporary, finite, and corruptible. They wear out and break down. Cars break down and lose value. Homes age and require repairs. Homes can catch fire, flood, or get destroyed by a number of natural disasters such as hurricanes and tornadoes. Jewelry breaks, gets lost, or stolen. The latest technology is outdated in a few short years or even months. Material possessions require ongoing replenishment which can send people on a downward spiral financially, emotionally, and psychologically. The pursuit of possessions becomes a never-ending exercise of acquiring, fixing, replacing, and spending that never fulfills what is missing in our lives. Because material things are of this world, they are corruptible and subject to Satan's influence.

The enemy wants to steal from you. Satan can't take God's love from you but he can take away all the material worldly things you have. Because worldly possessions are temporary and finite, having a love for such things can lead a person down a treacherous path. This is what the enemy wants from you. He wants to draw you away from God to win you over through selfish desires. Placing all our trust in the pursuit of material things will lead to a life of worry. Worry that we don't have enough things. It will lead to anxiety. Being anxious about losing what possessions we have and not having what we think we want. Material things can never fill the God-shaped void in our hearts so we will always feel unfulfilled when pursuing such things.

I was told recently by someone that real estate is constant and you can count on it. To which I replied, there are homes and properties right here in Florida that now reside at the bottom of a sinkhole. There are neighborhoods that no longer exist because the hill they were on was swept away in a mudslide. Beachfront property can be washed away by storms. Not even real estate is constant. One can argue that is what insurance is for. But insurance only replaces the value of the real estate in the form of money, which is not constant as we read earlier. Insurance doesn't replace the physical land that is at the bottom of a sinkhole or was washed out to the sea during a big storm. Insurance just replaces one finite, temporary object with another.

It becomes very clear that when you replace the steadfast, ever-present, constant love of God (L^3) with temporary, finite, corruptible material possessions ($M_P^{\$}$), our faith as a foundation for our principles fails at every level. It is not the amount of money in our bank account or the number of fancy possessions here on earth by which we are measured. It is how much treasure one has built up in heaven through faith in Jesus Christ and exemplifying the love and kindness of Jesus throughout our lives that is measured by God. By praying over the equation $F = TL^3$, you can focus on what you do have and that is God's love for you and Jesus Christ as your savior. God's love can never be taken away and should never be replaced as the number one primary focus of all our trust.

CHAPTER 7

LEAD WELL

F = $T(P_L^{\wedge})^{\wedge}$: Faith equals trust times power and leadership. Power can be pursued at many levels. Power can be sought out at federal and local government levels. Power can be sought out at work, in the home, and even on the playground at school. When power becomes the primary focus and pursuit, sought after at the expense of other people and at the expense of freedom, it can and usually does become a problem.

> **"But select capable men from all the people—men who fear God, trustworthy men who hate dishonest gain—and appoint them as officials over thousands, hundreds, fifties and tens."**
>
> **(EXODUS 18:21 NIV)**

Like money, power is not evil in and of itself. We need leaders. God has placed leaders of people all through the Bible. Moses had to appoint capable men to help him oversee the issues that the Israelites faced in the wilderness. Abraham, Joshua, Jacob, David, and many more were all leaders. Leadership is a God-given gift to many and quality leadership is a valuable trait. It is so important for leaders to lead from a God-centered place. That means lead with compassion, wisdom, and love. God's love is a great source of inspiration for all leaders.

People need to be careful, though. Power is not a constant; it is temporary, finite, fleeting, and very corruptible. Power should not be at the core of your pursuit. Leaders come and go. Leaders are made peaceably and leaders are made violently. When leaders seek power for the sake of power, they tend to make decisions selfishly. They are just trying to protect their position and have no regard for the people they are leading. By placing all your trust in the pursuit of power, you will fail at properly leading those around you. You will fail at building a sound foundational faith.

Having power typically goes hand in hand with being in a position of leadership. I define a successful leader as someone who leads by example, leads from compassion, and leads by serving those being led. I believe Jesus was the perfect leader. Pastor Matt Blair calls this servant leadership. He often says, "If you are too big to serve, then you are too small to lead." Pastor Matt gets into the trenches with everyone who serves at Limitless Church. This is such an important facet of leadership that Pastor Matt has made it one of the church's core values: Servant leadership is our calling.

Jesus leads by example. **"For to this you were called, because Christ also suffered for you, leaving you an example, so that you might follow in his steps. He committed no sin, neither was deceit found in his mouth" (1 Peter 2:21–22 ESV).** Jesus lived a sinless, exemplary life while here on earth. Jesus set the example by which all should follow. As a leader of others, I have tried very hard to follow this example, yet I seem to fall far short of it. We all fall short of perfection because we are only human. Leaders must continue to remind themselves that the people they lead are watching. People want to know that their leaders have been in their shoes and can do what they are being asked to do. The example a leader sets will set the tone for those being led. Leaders that focus on selfish needs and desires like money and more promotions at the expense of hurting those around them set a poor tone for success. Those being led will experience fear and anxiety. This will lead to a lack of productivity. The people being led will not perform at their best. How can a person focus on being the best they can be when they are under undue fear and anxiety? I find that I do my best work in an environment where I am focused on the task at hand, not when fear or anxiety shares that focus and steals energy away from the work that needs to be done. The most effective leaders serve as an example to those they lead. They are humble yet confident.

"Do nothing from selfish ambition or conceit, but in humility count others more significant than yourselves. Let each of you look not only to his own interests, but also to the interests of others."

(**PHILIPPIANS 2:3-4** ESV)

Jesus led with a compassionate and forgiving heart. **"Be kind and compassionate to one another, forgiving each other, just as Christ God forgave you" (Ephesians 4:32 NIV).** Jesus teaches us to love our enemies and pray for those who persecute us. Leaders need to lead from a place of compassion and empathy for those they lead. This will give the leader a better view of where those being led are standing. We all live lives that seem to have their fair share of drama, strife, and aggravations. Knowing this as a leader can help to understand that these things do bleed over into the workplace. A leader can then get a better understanding of what is perhaps hurting performance and then walk through it with that person. Talk it out. Be a compassionate, understanding leader. Leaders will get so much more out of those they lead.

As a leader, I feel it would be a success if I were told by those I lead that "They just want to be their best because I make them feel that they are at their best even if they are not there yet." It takes time to develop good talent. If, in a reasonable amount of time, the employee is not working out, then it may be time to change course from coaching up to coaching out. A great leader once told me that sometimes it is best to help an employee find their happiness elsewhere. A good leader can recognize when there is just a bad fit with a particular employee. I don't believe in raising my voice in the workplace or even at home for that matter. I have never yelled at an employee or degraded them for doing a poor job. I believe in compassionately coaching people up to do their best.

This goes for children as well. Parents are leaders too. Parents lead their children through the first eighteen to twenty years of their young lives. Parenting from a place of compassion is vital to the success of children. Allowing anger and disappointment to cloud your judgment as a parent can lead to a child rebelling against authority—the authority of you, the parents, as well as teachers, law enforcement, and employers. I do believe in discipline but discipline derived wisely and compassionately.

We have all had a leader we just didn't like or respect; perhaps a teacher, boss, pastor, or parental figure. Think hard about what made that person such a negative influence in your life. I find that those were leaders that were angry all the time, put people down, bullied, and lead out of their own selfish needs and desires. I would classify these individuals as "failures" at leadership regardless of how much money they made or how important others thought they were.

I worked for an individual years ago who constantly threatened me with my job and antagonized me for not selling the specific products that paid him the biggest bonus. He would come to my office and bully me, saying I would be the next one fired if I didn't move certain products. Products that were just not suitable for the clients I represented. I would always tell him that the particular product just wasn't suitable for my clients. He would always reply, "Suitable or not, I need my bonus this month!" I always refused and would leave the office at the end of the day wrestling with anxiety and fear over losing my job. I was never actually fired over my refusal to sell certain products, but that didn't diminish the feelings of fear and anxiety I experienced regularly. Protecting his position and pursuing more power and leadership opportunities was the focus of this leader. That pursuit came at the expense of others. Most of us working in that office did not like or respect this him at all.

"In the same way, let your light shine before others, so that they may see your good works and give glory to your Father who is in heaven."

(MATTHEW 5:16 ESV)

Several years later, I worked for a leader who was the complete opposite. This leader always encouraged me to do what was in my client's best interest; to walk away from the sale if it wasn't the best thing for the client. When I made mistakes, he would call me into his office, not to berate me, but to compassionately explain where I had made the mistake and then offer solutions to prevent future mistakes. I have a tremendous amount of respect for this leader and would follow him anywhere. I wanted to succeed just to please him. He got just as much pleasure from the success of those he led as they did. Doesn't God derive pleasure from our good fortune? Of course, he does; he is the giver. The leader mentioned in this paragraph is leading by Jesus' example. He may not do it perfectly but he does do it well. I am not the only one who feels this way, there are hundreds of people who feel the same way about this particular leader across my organization.

Power and leadership has never been the focus of this leader. He has always, as long as I have known him, cared more about those he lead than his own success. This style of leadership also impacts how leaders under him lead as well. He is responsible for a caring, forgiving, compassionate culture that reaches most markets around the country for this organization. It is no secret as to why the organization has been wildly successful for so many years.

It is so important to show those being led that you do forgive their mistakes and shortcomings so they don't hold resentment. After all, leaders make mistakes as well. Those we lead can see those mistakes. By forgiving and coaching through the mistakes and wrongdoings of others, a leader can quickly earn the respect and favor of those being led. It is important to offer constructive solutions when dealing with mistakes. If the mistake is so business critical that termination of employment is required, delivering the termination using a respectful tone of voice and showing empathy toward the person being terminated will go a long way and even ease the stress of the employee being terminated. This will lead to loyalty and a true desire to succeed in the hearts and minds of people being led. Praying over the equation $F = TL^3$ when leading others and making leadership decisions will help to remind a leader that it is God's love that guides us. It is the example we see in Christ's love for us that should direct a leader down the right path.

Now that we understand how leadership goes hand in hand with power, let's look more closely at how the equation $F = T(P_L^\wedge)$ fails as a foundational equation for faith. There are many infamous leaders in history who pursued power above all things including human life. Ivan the Terrible, Adolf Hitler, Idi Amin, Pol Pot, and Saddam Hussein are but a few of the most notorious leaders in history. These leaders used torture and murder as tools to breed fear in people. They used this fear to control the masses, believing it would help them keep hold of their power. This is just an illusion, however, and led to their ultimate downfall as leaders. These leaders were not the first to corrupt power.

"Because I know the evil that you will do to the people of Israel. You will set on fire their fortresses, and you will kill their young men with the sword and dash in pieces their little ones and rip open their pregnant women."

(2 KINGS 8:12 ESV)

The Bible gives many examples of power's corruptibility. The First and Second Books of Kings describe forty kings, thirty-eight of which chose to lead in the absence of God's love and corrupted the power that they were given. As a result, their power ended in many cases quite violently. Some of the kings reigned for just a few years. Their reign of power was very brief. The Bible gives us many glaring examples of what it looks like to lead outside of God's love, corrupting and misusing the power given by God. The outcome is always less than desirable.

All the power these leaders had was just temporary and finite. Their power ended violently for most of them. They reaped what they sowed. These men thought that their power would be the pinnacle of their pursuit. Power was not the constant they thought it would be as each leader's reign of power always comes to an end. The one true constant that never ends is God's love for us.

We see this style of leadership in our everyday lives, not just in the headlines and history books. There are employers who use fear to try to keep employees down. There are parents who use brutality and fear to raise their children. There are bullies on the playground and in schools who do the same. These are all examples of people pursuing power over others at an extreme cost.

Bullying is the pursuit of power through abusive means, whether physical, verbal, emotional or psychological. We see it at work, in homes, and in schools. This is not a godly way to pursue power. We need leaders who pursue power and leadership through God's love. $F = TL^3$ is an equation for leaders. Employers can use this equation for effective leadership in the workplace. Effective leadership leads to efficiencies that will help a company to be more profitable. By leading lovingly and compassionately, businesses can operate in God's economy. God's economy is the most profitable economy of all. The sole pursuit of power in the workplace can be and usually is detrimental to others. Even if you get that promotion or raise, it just won't last. Eventually, leaders are replaced and the money earned is spent. There is nothing constant in the equation $F = T(P^\wedge_L)$ and the pursuit of power before God ultimately leaves us unfulfilled. Power will never fill the emptiness in your heart like the love of God.

"Start children off on the way they should go, and even when they are old they will not turn from it."

(Proverbs 22:6 NIV)

Parenting is one of the most important and difficult jobs we may have in life. As parents, we are in a position of power and leadership. The example we set as parents is very important and leading through God's love as a parent is vital. A parent has the ability to mold a child from a God-shaped mold or from some mold much less desirable. Parents who use the wrong equation, one that uses P_L as a false constant, can cause a tremendous amount of damage to a child. We see this all the time. The foster care system is overrun with children who have been removed from abusive and neglectful homes. Perverting power as a parent and using it abusively will lead to failure. Abused children end up, in many cases, turning to a life of crime, drug, and alcohol addiction and repeating the cycle of abuse with their children.

"No discipline seems pleasant at the time, but painful. Later on, however, it produces a harvest of righteousness and peace for those who have been trained by it."

(HEBREWS 12:11 NIV)

Parents who lead their children through God's love can be sure that their children will have the best chance of becoming a well-rounded, secure adult. This is certainly not to say that raising a child through God's love is raising a child without discipline. Discipline is foundational for a child's development. There is a balance when it comes to discipline; it needs to be just but not abusive. Disciplining from a place of compassion and love will yield the best results. Parents don't need to beat their children to get them to behave well. Physical abuse can cause more problems than it solves. The scars of physical abuse will run far deeper than what we see on the surface. Abuse can lead to deep emotional and psychological scars.

The physical abuse and neglect we often see parents perpetrating on to their kids comes from believing in the power of being a parent justifies the abuse and neglect. Putting the term P_L in place of God's love in our equation allows a parent to wrongfully justify the abuse of a child. God's love would never allow for such a justification. Placing our trust in our power as a parent will lead us to failing as a parent.

Bullying among our youth is a growing problem in our country. Kids bully at school and on social media. This kind of bullying can lead to extreme behavior on the part of those being bullied. We read in the headlines that a child committed suicide because of being picked on and bullied. Children who have been bullied have gone into schools and murdered their classmates. These are extreme outcomes but are becoming more and more prevalent in our society. This is where the equation

$F = TL^3$ can be used to teach kids the power of God's love for them. Children can focus on God's love giving them a greater sense of security and self-worth. Many times, children lash out at other kids out of feelings of insecurity. Perhaps they are ignored by their parents or even abused at home. By showing a child just how much God loves him or her, perhaps he or she will realize their own value.

As a parent, I have met many of my children's friends. I have found through my own experience that the kids who feel secure and sense their own self-worth are not likely to bully other kids at all. The power of God's love has the ability to reveal to a child his or her self-worth. When a child places their trust in the love of God, they don't need to try to lift themselves up by putting others down. They feel secure in who they are as children of God. Parents are responsible for teaching their children that they are truly loved and this equation can be a simple illustration to assist in that process.

Pray for your children daily: *"Father God, please give me the wisdom to help my child have the knowledge and understanding that you love him/ her so much that you died on the cross so that he/she may live. As the Holy Spirit pours your love through me and directly into him/her, please bring your love to the forefront of their being so he/she feels secure in your love and knows his/her worth."* This is a simple yet powerful prayer that is based on the equation $F = TL^3$. Praying for our children is very important in our walk as Christians. Praying with our children is also very important and will increase the personal impact prayer has on each of their lives.

Replacing God's love (L^3) with fleeting, finite, and corruptible term *power* and *leadership* (P_L) in the equation for faith fails time and time again. The term (P_L) is just not a suitable value on which to build your faith and ultimately your principles. Power can be dangerous if pursued recklessly. We as Christians can positively affect our leaders through prayer. Pray for the wisdom and compassion of our leaders every day. Pray they make decisions reflective of God's plans and not their own. Through these prayers, it is my hope that all the leaders at every point in our lives lead through Christ Jesus.

CHAPTER 8

THE ROOT

S elfishness is the root of all sin. **"For all have sinned and fall short of the glory of God, and all are justified freely by his grace through the redemption that came by Christ Jesus" (Romans 3:23–24 NIV).**

$F = TS^3$ Faith equals trust times self cubed (me, myself, and I). I have found that a lot of people prefer to place all their trust in themselves rather than God. Many people put themselves before God. They put their trust in their own intellect, abilities, and even feelings. They attempt to control every aspect of their lives. These are people who lean on phrases such as: *"If it is not done right, do it yourself." "If at first you don't succeed, try, try again." "God helps those who help themselves."* (God never said that.) *"Only you are in control of your own destiny."* This is a lonely and stressful way to live. The enemy wants to lead you into a false sense of security in yourself that will lead you away from God. It is difficult to see God when you are not looking beyond yourself. When you are focused inwardly, wrapped up so intently in yourself, putting God and others first is extremely difficult. The enemy wants you to blind yourself in your own self-worth, allowing you to think you are above and before all else.

Of course, a little selfishness is required for survival. We all have to feed ourselves and clothe ourselves. God will provide what we need such as food, clothing, and shelter, but we still need to pick up the food and put it in our mouths. We still need to put on the clothes God provides. It is important to treat the self and body well. We need to exercise regularly and eat nutritious food for our health and well-being. After all, our body is a temple of the Holy Spirit and it does us well to keep it in good working condition. God has not called us to be so selfless that we completely ignore ourselves to the point we deteriorate and die. That is not the point of this chapter. The point is to understand that we are broken, sinful beings who need God's love so desperately.

"Whoever trusts in his own mind is a fool, but he who walks in wisdom will be delivered."

(PROVERBS 28:26 ESV)

Why is placing trust in one's self potentially so dangerous? Because as people we are all flawed, broken sinners capable of making mistakes. No one is perfect. No one is right 100% of the time. No one goes through life "batting a thousand." The only person deserving of that honor is Jesus Christ. We are all destined to fail from time to time. Misunderstandings and misinterpretations are at the core of being human and lead to making poor judgments and poor decisions.

Every person reading these pages has had many misunderstandings and made many mistakes throughout their lives. It is part of being human. Our minds play tricks on us all the time. We hear what we think we hear, see what we think we see, and as a result, get it wrong quite often.

"All day long they twist my words; all their schemes are for my ruin."

(PSALM 56:5 NIV)

Have you ever had a misunderstanding about a conversation at work? You only hear a few parts of a conversation but come to a conclusion and make a comment that is out of context. What was the result? Perhaps it resulted in receiving strange looks from your coworkers or even an argument. Whatever the result, it probably was not a positive one.

How about at home? Have you ever misunderstood your spouse or children? Did it result in an argument or some other negative outcome? My guess is, yes, it did. Recently, my wife entered the room where my daughter and I were watching television. She had a raised voice and was clearly upset that my daughter had not completed her chores before sitting down to watch TV, or so I thought. The TV volume was up rather loud as my hearing is not great. So, when I believed I heard my wife chastising our daughter for not completing her chores, I thought she was overreacting with her raised voice. I was under the impression she was very angry and was yelling at her for this particular situation. This caused me to react in a way that would be very inconsistent with how I should have reacted if I really understood my wife's comments and intentions. My wife was not yelling out of anger, she was only trying to speak over the volume of the TV. She wasn't even chastising our daughter for not yet having done her chores. She was merely asking if they had been done yet. I clearly misinterpreted my wife's comments and overall intentions.

My reaction being somewhat defensive started an argument and caused my wife to feel hurt. She was also upset that it did not appear the two of us were a united front in the eyes of our daughter. My wife and I spent a few days with a cloud of tension over us as a result of my misunderstanding. I placed my trust in my own understanding of the situation and I got it very wrong. Husbands, if you are at all like me, you know this is not a pleasant experience in a marriage, yet we have all experienced it. Misunderstandings and misinterpretations like this happen all the time in relationships. The ability of our minds to misunderstand different situations is just one example of how we are flawed and how the equation $F = TS^3$ can fail at producing a sound value for our faith.

"But Jesus answered them, 'You are wrong, because you know neither the Scriptures nor the power of God.'"

(MATTHEW 22:29 ESV)

Why do we misinterpret? Why do we misunderstand? The answer lies within our experiences. Each person has a vastly different set of experiences throughout each of their lives. Each person also has a very unique brain that interprets and translates those experiences differently from others as well.

Each of us has an understanding of the world around us based primarily on the sphere of or set of experiences we each encounter throughout our lives. This sphere of experience is unique to every man, woman, and child on the planet. Imagine drawing a circle, and in that circle, you place every experience you have ever had up to this very moment in time and represents your sphere of experience, and all the experiences you never had fall outside the circle.

For example: I studied the martial arts for many years and have experienced physical combat with another person in the ring at a tournament and even just while training. The experience of physical combat in a martial arts tournament would be an experience that I would place inside my circle. However, I was never a member of our armed forces and have never been in military combat. I have never experienced the fear, the sounds, the smells, the stress of putting my life in harm's way by fighting for my country. I don't know what it is like knowing that around every corner I turn, there could be a bomb or enemy with a gun pointed at me. This would be an experience that falls outside of my circle. I have experienced combat, combat in a structured format within the parameters of a sport. I have not experienced military combat.

I refer to the edge of the circle as the "Experiential Event Horizon." An event horizon is "a boundary beyond which events cannot affect an observer on the opposite side of it" (Wikipedia 2019). In astronomy it refers to the theoretical boundary around a black hole beyond which no light or radiation can escape. The Experiential Event Horizon is a boundary that encapsulates all the experiences of an individual. Beyond which are all the possible experiences an individual has never encountered, hence has little to no effect on an individual.

Our experiences influence the decisions we make. Our brains were designed to learn from our experiences and help us make better decisions as a result of what we learn. However, we can and often do come to irrational conclusions from our experience. We develop irrational fears that can be paralyzing. We become angry and lash out at others over very benign actions. When another driver accidentally cuts in front of us closer than we think they should have, we respond with: "You should have seen me... Are you Blind?" The fact is that most close calls on the road ways happen completely by accident. The other driver whether distracted or not had no idea just how close they got. Our inward focus on ourselves causes us to interpret the world around us as if it revolves around us. Our selfishness and insecurities become magnified and as a result our understanding become less and less trustworthy. When we turn our focus off ourselves and onto God, we see through God's eyes, we can feel His spirit. It is through the Holy Spirit that we get a better understanding of the world around us because it is God's understanding. Through God's understanding irrational fears and anxiety melt away. We become better people when we rely on God over ourselves which is a pleasant side effect of that immense love.

Since every person experiences the world differently, how can we truly trust the decisions we make? We simply have to try to use our best judgment based on our own set of experiences. For example, someone who may have had a close encounter with a shark while swimming in the ocean might decide to never swim in the ocean again. Conversely, someone who has not had the same close encounter would be willing to swim in the ocean anytime. What makes this important and illustrates the effects on our ability to make decisions are as follows: Neither swimmer in the example above is any more likely to be bitten by a shark than the other. Each swimmer has, statistically, the same chance of being bitten by a shark if they enter the water the same number of times. However, each swimmer makes a decision to enter the water based on their past experiences. One swimmer has developed a fear of the ocean due to a close encounter with a shark and the other has not. The ocean, though, is no more dangerous for either of the two swimmers than the other. Just because one swimmer saw a shark doesn't make the water any more dangerous than any other day that swimmer chose to swim. The experience of visually seeing a shark in the water has changed the understanding or perception of the amount of danger the ocean represents for that person. It didn't change how dangerous the ocean actually is.

Two people can have different experiences even though they are in close proximity to one another. Being just a few feet apart can shift the experience between two people completely. Now let's assume the two swimmers are both in the water just a few feet apart at the same time and the shark makes an appearance. One swimmer sees the shark and is aware of its presence and the other swimmer does not. The swimmer who saw the shark hightails it back to shore while the other swimmer calmly swims on, perhaps thinking, *Wow, that guy must have to use the bathroom badly.* After the shark swims away without incident, the two swimmers will probably make very similar decisions as the two above. The swimmer who saw the shark decides to never go in the ocean again while the other swimmer has no problem even going swimming again that very same day. These two decisions are just two out of a wide array of many possible decisions. This is just to illustrate how two people might come to two very different conclusions about the danger in the ocean despite being in the same general location and despite the fact that the ocean is statistically no more dangerous for either swimmer.

> **"So do not fear, for I am with you; do not be dismayed, for I am your God. I will strengthen you and help you; I will uphold you with my righteous right hand."**
>
> **(ISAIAH 41:10 NIV)**

Since God sees all, he sees the experiences of all people simultaneously. God knows what is going to happen before it happens and he knows the consequences as well. If this is the case, then God would be the best being to follow when we make decisions. By placing all our trust in God's love, we can easily see the wisdom in following his plan for us rather than our own. The equation $F = TL^3$ helps us know that God has this because he loves us so intently.

"'For I know the plans I have for you,' declares the Lord, 'plans to prosper you and not to harm you, plans to give you hope and a future.'"

(JEREMIAH 29:11 NIV)

"Give thanks in all circumstances; for this is God's will for you in Christ Jesus."

(1 THESSALONIANS 5:18 NIV)

We see the same type of decision-making process of the swimmers when it comes to faith. A person who lives a relatively good life, does well financially, and has a good family might feel they don't need God in their lives. Everything is going fine without him. This individual thinks he himself has this and is ultimately trusting in his own abilities. Another person who has had some struggles and pain in their life might look to God to help them through those tough times. This individual may choose to put some amount of trust in God to assist him through the difficult time rather than trusting their own abilities. Perhaps the tough times have been a wake-up call for this person, showing him the error of his ways of trying to do it without God. Just because these two people have had different experiences and have a different understanding of how much or how little they need God and God's love in their lives based on those experiences doesn't change the fact that they both need God equally. The understanding they come to based on their experiences doesn't change the fact that they both need God in their lives. Those experiences only change their perception of the need. Therein lies the danger. Misunderstanding the need for God's love in your life and following a path leading away from God will have devastating consequences.

"But seek first the kingdom of God and his righteousness, and all these things will be added to you."

(Matthew 6:33 ESV)

Placing one's self before God leads to making poor decisions. I have spoken to many people who tell me they don't need to attend church. They tell me they know their relationship with God. Or they don't need God because they themselves have everything in control. Pastor Matt Blair of Limitless Church in Tampa, Florida preaches regularly that, as Christians, we were not meant to do this alone. We do need the church because we need the Body of Christ. We need to interact with the Body of Christ. The Body of Christ is where you find two or more people in worship and prayer with Jesus. Church for many Christians is where we find that Body of Christ on a regular basis. The church is more than just Sunday services. Through a church, you can also find the Body of Christ in small groups throughout the week—people gathering outside of Sunday services coming together in prayer, worship, support, and friendship. Some of the best friends I have are the friends I meet with regularly in small groups. So to think I am so great that I can do this all on my own is a poor decision at best. It would be a very lonely walk through life if I didn't have my family at Limitless Church to pray and worship with each and every Sunday as well as in small groups throughout the week.

The equation $F = TL^3$ can help us to understand the need for the Body of Christ. By knowing and trusting in the triune love of God, we can feel God's love poured into us through the Holy Spirit. As a result we can see the importance of pouring that love back out into those around us. If we try to do this on our own we won't have anyone to pour that love into. We will completely miss the command to love our neighbor—an outwardly focused act.

Since love is an outward focusing act, placing trust in one's self before God is completely inward focusing. It is an inward focus on one's self. Selfishness is a sin because it does not represent true love—it can't. Love has to be given and given freely, therefore, by definition, love of the self is just holding on to something, hoarding something that should be poured out into others. It is completely inwardly focused. Perhaps people behave this way because they were hurt by someone in the past. Again, this is a poor decision based on past experiences. Don't stop loving others just because you have been hurt in the past. Don't stop loving God just because you perceive you will be hurt again. People will hurt you and people will fail you. You will hurt others and you will fail others because that is human nature. Human nature tells us that we are not the rock solid basis for faith that God's love is.

> **"Therefore be imitators of God, as beloved children. And walk in love, as Christ loved us and gave himself up for us, a fragrant offering and sacrifice to God."**
>
> **(EPHESIANS 5:1–2 ESV)**

We are all flawed and imperfect. God, however, is not. God continues to love each of us knowing the risk of rejection. He has experienced that since Adam and Eve. When we love each other with full knowledge and understanding of the risk of being hurt or rejected, we are reflecting God's love and that is one of God's greatest desires. Like the moon reflecting the light of the sun, we reflect the love of the Son when we freely love others. So, pray over the equation $F = TL^3$ and make the decision to reflect the love of Jesus Christ; making the right decision, a decision uninfluenced by worldly experiences.

> **"Jesus answered them, 'Truly, truly, I say to you, everyone who practices sin is a slave to sin."**
>
> **(JOHN 8:34 ESV)**

Selfishness is the root of all sin because all sin is derived by focusing on self-satisfaction, self-gratification, personal gain, self-importance, and by honing in so intently on one's own self. This is the polar opposite of love as love is purely a focus on God and others. When we love God and others, we are not focused on ourselves, we focus outwardly. God's greatest desire is for us to love him with all our heart, mind, and soul, and to love others as we would ourselves. Nowhere does God ask us to put ourselves first.

> **"Do not let your adorning be external—the braiding of hair and the putting on of gold jewelry, or the clothing you wear— but let your adorning be the hidden person of the heart with the imperishable beauty of a gentle and quiet spirit..."**
>
> **(1 Peter 3:3–4 ESV)**

The desire for beauty can be a selfish desire, therefore it fits well as an additional example for this chapter. $F = T(B_v)$: Faith equals trust times physical beauty and vanity. To think that beauty can be represented as a constant in term in a faith equation is quite absurd. Physical beauty is anything but constant. The aging process makes sure of that. People can spend years pursuing a state of physical beauty, but ultimately, time wins out. The entropic principle ensures that we will age and our youthful good looks will fade away. There are many equations used to calculate the dynamic qualities of this theory. Entropy is described in the second law of thermodynamics. The second law of thermodynamics states: in an irreversible process, entropy always increases. Entropy represents the amount of disorder in a system. As we age, which at last check is irreversible, the organization of cells and their structures become more and more disordered causing the process we see as aging. Our skin starts to sag and wrinkle, we lose our hair or it turns gray, our organs start to fail and we develop diseases such as cancer. This is an inescapable process no matter how much money or time we invest in our physical beauty. All attempts to slow the process visually are just temporary. We will all lose the battle with time and entropy. One formula for entropy is represented as $dU = dq + dw$. Solving for entropy is unnecessary for the purpose of this book. Another example I'll show because I think it looks cool represents the total energy in a microstate: $E = \sum_{j=0}^{\infty} {}^{\wedge}n_j E_j$. An example of entropy could be described as follows: Take a book like *War and Peace* by Tolstoy which has 1,225 pages. The book in its bound form with all the pages in order from page 1 to page 1,225 is in a state of low entropy because it is in perfect order. Now, imagine slicing the spine of the book off so all the pages would be loose and throwing it up in the air. The resulting mix of jumbled pages would represent a higher state of entropy as the pages are now out of order. If you were to continue to pick up the pages and repeat the process of throwing them up in the air, the result would be a greater degree of disorder or a higher state of entropy as the pages became more and more out of their original order. As we age, our cells go through a somewhat similar process causing what we see as aging.

The pursuit of physical beauty can manifest itself into a serious problem for some people. It is not so much that desiring to be beautiful is bad because it isn't. As a matter of fact, the word beauty appears in the Bible over one hundred times. It is when that desire consumes us that it causes problems. Beauty is subjective. It means something different to everyone. The phrase "Beauty is in the eye of the beholder" describes this concept. So, if beauty is subjective and represents something different to everyone, then what exactly is it that we as people are chasing after? Is it the standard we see portrayed in magazines, movies, and on television? If so, then that is flawed for who are the media executives to tell us what true beauty is? Also, it only represents the surface appearance, how we look physically. Humans are visual creatures and I get why we are so attracted to the things that look visually pleasing. However, this is not where true beauty emanates from. True beauty comes from within. It represents the person's heart, soul, and mind.

"Charm is deceitful, and beauty is vain, but a woman who fears the Lord is to be praised."

(PROVERBS 31:30 ESV)

By pursuing so intently the physical attributes of beauty, we completely miss the mark. We believe, "If I was just prettier, thinner, tanner, more muscular, had better hair, etc., that life would be better. Perhaps I could get a better job, get that raise or promotion, have more friends, or get a husband or wife." These are just lies that the enemy wants you to believe. But we believe the lies and spend thousands of dollars and countless hours pursuing something that doesn't even translate the same way to those around us as we think it does for us. People are willing to risk their health in the pursuit of beauty. They will inject steroids to build muscle artificially at the risk of getting cancer and having cardiovascular issues later in life. They will endure risky cosmetic surgeries that have been known to severely mutilate their appearance and even cause death. They will starve themselves, developing severe mental health issues that can lead to death such as anorexia. Why do we do this? Because we desire attention and affection and we believe physical beauty will deliver on that. But trying to obtain these things as a means of fulfillment through beauty is nothing more than a huge lie. Beauty comes from the heart and resides in love and compassion for others.

When we replace God's love (L^3) in equations such as $F = TS^3$ and $F = T(B_v)$, the equations fail on every point as placing all trust in the self or beauty is an extreme inwardly focused lifestyle. This extreme inward focus leads to selfishness and leads toward more idolatry. Placing one's self first before God is all about satisfying selfish desires through self-gratification and self-satisfaction. You will want more and more that satisfies the self like money, power, material possessions, beauty, and admiration. The self is by far the most dangerous of terms to try and build a faith on. The extreme pressure and stress one puts themselves under constantly trying to keep up with finite, temporary, limited, and corruptible worldly things is exhausting. I myself have tried living like this when I was younger and I can't remember a time when I was more anxious unfulfilled and downright unhappy.

CHAPTER 9

FAILURE HAPPENS

F $= T(C_L^\wedge)$: Faith equals trusting in our church leaders as if they were God himself. This is a path to certain pain and disappointment that can cause "church hurt." I have spoken to many people over the past few years who no longer attend church or no longer believe in God because they were hurt by a pastor or member of a church. I would always ask how the act of being hurt by a pastor or church member could lead them away from God. The answer is usually, "These are people of God. They, of all people, should show complete love and tolerance for their parishioners. How could they do evil of any kind? How could God allow that?" To which I usually respond, "Pastors, priests, church leaders of any kind are people *first*. They are broken, imperfect sinners like you and I. Just because God has called someone into ministry doesn't cure them of their imperfections. Furthermore, just because someone has chosen to be a church leader doesn't mean that it is God's plan for that person. Perhaps they are forcing themselves into a plan that God did not intend for them."

"No temptation has overtaken you that is not common to man."

(1 CORINTHIANS 10:13 ESV)

When we place trust in our church leaders like how we place trust in God, we are holding them up to expectations they just can't maintain. Because your pastor is human, he or she will disappoint you. Your pastor will fail you from time to time. A church leader is no more immune to making mistakes and sinning than you are or I am. So why do we take it so personally when a church leader sins against us or the community? Because we have wrongly placed too much trust in someone who is no less human than the rest of us. Church leaders can be corrupted. All people can be corrupted. We all are capable of being lured into temptation through the desire for worldly things. Like you and I, a church leader can be tempted by money, power, sex, and material possessions. A church leader can have a bad day, be in a bad mood, and say things they wish they never said just like the rest of us. To think pastors, priests, and ministers are immune to all the attacks of the enemy is just not realistic.

So, to make the decision to pull away from God because of a bad experience you had with a church leader is yet another example of very poor judgment. It is another example of how we should not place so much trust in ourselves or others. God's love for us is unfailing and is the only thing we should place our trust in that won't fail us or hurt us. By making sure we always place God's love as the constant term in our faith equation, we can understand that church leaders are people too—capable of hurting and failing us. With our focus on God's love, we can then find it in our hearts to forgive those who hurt us. Remember, forgiveness is a product of love.

> **"Put on then, as God's chosen ones, holy and beloved, compassionate hearts, kindness, humility, meekness, and patience, bearing with one another and, if one has a complaint against another, forgiving each other; as the Lord has forgiven you, so you also must forgive."**
>
> **(Colossians 3:12–13 ESV)**

We don't need to turn our backs on God or the church when a church leader falls down or trips up. We need to know that they probably will and they need us as much as we need them. When we see our church leaders making mistakes, we as the Body of Christ need to let them know what they are doing is wrong and help them correct the problem. We need to love them and forgive them and reflect as much of Christ's love as we possibly can back on to them to make them better as leaders. Turning our back on someone who hurts us is a knee-jerk reaction. Turning our backs on God when a person hurts us is even worse and an act that God does not deserve.

God's love is the only thing that will never fail you and the only thing that follows you into heaven. Turning away from that due to worldly experiences is exactly what Satan wants you to do. Satan knows that we do place too much trust in our church leaders and that he can get to us through them. Don't let the enemy win. When and if you are hurt or disappointed by a church leader, pour more love and forgiveness into that person and fight the enemy's attack.

"I urge you, brothers and sisters, to watch out for those who cause divisions and put obstacles in your way that are contrary to the teaching you have learned. Keep away from them. For such people are not serving our Lord Christ, but their own appetites. By smooth talk and flattery they deceive the minds of naive people."

(ROMANS 16:17–18 NIV)

How do we identify church leaders who might be forcing their own will and not the will of God? I have found that it typically comes down to legalism and the absence of Jesus in the message. This typically manifests as a judgment and condemnation of people in a particular church versus the preaching of the Scripture to those people. The Word of God, the Bible, is the authority by which we know God loves us. If a church leader focuses the message around the written word of God, the Gospel of Christ, and on God's love for us all, then I believe you are in a good environment. But when leaders preach that you or others are being less of a Christian because you do or don't do certain things, and preach rules more so than the Gospel, I feel that is the wrong message. I truly believe we are all equally Christian by the fact we have chosen to accept the Gospels as truth. We have all accepted Jesus Christ as our savior. We are all just humans and can get lost along the way. As a result, we should all love each other and help each other find our way back to Christ when we lose our way.

"I appeal to you, brothers, by all the name of our Lord Jesus Christ, that all of you agree, and that there be no divisions among you, but that you be united in the same mind and in the same judgment."

(1 CORINTHIANS 1:10 ESV)

Quarreling and division in the church is a complete waste of time and is an example of the mistakes made by church leaders. Church division can and often does cause hurt in the church. There is no reason to judge others simply because they choose to worship God a little differently. When we allow fighting among Christians due to our differences, we are allowing Satan into our most sacred houses and it is he who divides us for his gain. As Christians, we must unite and be tolerant of our differences in order to win the war with the enemy. Catholics, Protestants, Lutherans, Baptists, Methodists, and other nondenominational churches need to set aside their differences and join arm in arm against the enemy through love. By placing all our trust in God and God's love, we can then pour that love out onto each other and unite in the name of Jesus Christ, casting out the enemy and shining light on the dark corners we have allowed into our places of worship.

Pastors and preachers that dole out judgment and choose to reject and condemn those in need of their help the most are probably in the wrong calling. They are more than likely forcing their personal will over

God's. Now, I am not referring to those leaders who fall for a moment and say things they probably regret saying in a heated moment. That is human nature and usually a mistake or a moment of poor judgment. I am referring to those church leaders who build a culture of intolerance and judgment of the less fortunate or just plain different. It is the "culture" that is developed and built that lends itself as being more of a cult than a Church of God and a Body of Christ. I am not passing judgment over those leaders. I am, however, expressing what I believe is not how I would like to be led. I prefer to receive the Word of God through the preaching of the Scripture. I prefer to be around those who are tolerant of diversity and pour out love over those in the greatest need. I prefer to hear a message of Jesus.

I have a friend, a single mom struggling to make ends meet. She has been in several abusive relationships and was estranged from her son's father. She told me about a time she was hurt by a former pastor. She told me that, one day, the pastor asked if he could call her up to the front of the congregation to which she agreed trustingly. When she got up on stage, the pastor, in front of her young son and the whole congregation, called her a "whore" for being a mother out of wedlock. He went on to preach about how she was an example of how not to live your life. One can only imagine how devastating and embarrassing that must have been. She was embarrassed for herself and her son who had to endure the ridicule of his mother in front of all those people. The mistake here was the pastor taking on the role of judge. This pastor should have simply loved my friend. This was an extreme example of "church hurt"—being judged and ridiculed by a pastor. I pray for the pastor in this story and hope he has been loved by his parishioners so much that they showed him how wrong that was and helped him to be a better Christian, how to be a better pastor.

My friend could have turned her back on God after that but she didn't. She started attending a different church and continued to grow in her faith and in her love and adoration for God and Christ. I regularly receive devotionals from her expressing her love for God. Her story is a story of strength—the strength of God's love and how it gave her the strength not to give up on Jesus. After all, Jesus wasn't the source of the pain. The pain and mistreatment came from a man. It came from a person capable of failure, capable of sin.

I seek a relationship with God because he seeks a relationship with me. I want to reflect that desire for a relationship with everyone I encounter. That requires tolerance and acceptance of differences, not judgment, intolerance, and condemnation. Tolerance and compassion are the traits I have seen in the most successful church leaders and followers of Christ around the world. I understand that God has given us the ability to judge and condemn, I just don't believe he has given us the license.

Rather than judging others, church leaders should be the best example that they can be.

"Let no one despise you for your youth, but set the believers an example in speech, in conduct, in love, in faith, in purity" (1 Timothy 4:12 ESV). Church leaders need to understand that they are in the spotlight and Satan wants them to falter. They have to be aware of how well they are walking in the footsteps of Jesus Christ. If they don't, Satan will use that to pull believers away from the Body of Christ and away from God.

We all, as Christians, are ambassadors for Christ and as such are leaders. We are meant to lead by example, the example Jesus set for us. We all need to be aware of the Christlike example we try to set for others. We need to be compassionate, tolerant, and loving. Nonbelievers will use our poor example as Christians against us and twist it into an argument against God and against the church.

A few years ago, I was serving on the parking team and was assigned a position at the entrance of the church parking lot. That day, there was a man on a bicycle riding down the road toward the church when one of our parishioners nearly hit the cyclist as he turned onto the main road into the path of the man on the bike. The parishioner kept driving and turned into the church parking lot. The man on the bike was clearly upset and began screaming in anger about his close call. He said the driver had to have seen him and was being a horrible Christian for ignoring the incident and not being concerned for his safety. The reality was that the driver of the car had no idea that he had almost hit the cyclist. As a result, he had no idea that stopping was even necessary. This person chose to twist this event into something it wasn't because it happened in front of the church and involved a parishioner. The man on the bike would hear nothing of the truth and promptly called the police to report the near accident. Since there was no actual collision and no one was hurt, the police had no reason to come. That didn't deter the bicyclist from continuing to make a scene and denouncing the church because we must all be evil to stand behind such an evil and reckless driver. It is vitally important to be the best example we can be. We will never be perfect, and you can be sure that nonbelievers will make as much noise about it as they can when we fail.

It is easy to see that placing too much faith in our church leaders can lead to pain. We have to be very careful to realize our pastors and priests are just people too. They are prone to mistakes and capable of sinning. Making sure we are truly placing all our trust in God's love through the equation $F = TL^3$ will help us to avoid the mistake of assuming our church leaders are perfect; so when they do fail us, we can just love them where they are and help them to correct and overcome their mistakes.

For all the pastors, preachers, priests, and ministers who have tripped up, made mistakes, failed their flocks, I pray that you place all your trust in the fullness of God's love so that the people you lead will reflect that very same love. Father, give our church leaders the wisdom to speak true the Word of God, the Gospel, with tolerance and acceptance for all who need God's love regardless of their sinful ways.

CHAPTER 10

THE ATHEIST

$F = T(A_n^{\wedge})$: Faith equals trust multiplied by atheism's nothing. In this expression the capital "A" represents atheism, and the lowercase "n" represents the idea of nothing after death. Most staunch atheists I know believe that when we die, there is nothing. Our existence just comes to a definitive end, it is just over. I was an atheist for a little more than forty-two years. I placed all my trust in the belief that there was no God, no Jesus, no heaven or hell, and no life after death at all. I believed there was nothing after death. The idea was bleak. Contemplating the incredibly brief time we spend alive on earth, struggling day by day just to survive only to end up in a vacuous blackness void of all consciousness was actually very depressing. I felt very alone when really thinking about it. In my stubbornness, I stuck to this belief in light of its shortcomings for many years. Many atheists do the same and stubbornly hang on to this sad and very empty belief.

Many Christians have heard the argument about being right or wrong when it comes to atheism. The argument goes as follows: If the Christian, who believes in God and accepts Christ, is wrong and there is no heaven or hell, then he won't know the difference and in the end lose nothing for believing as, after death, he wouldn't even be conscious of the outcome. But if the atheist, who does not believe in God and does not accept Christ, is wrong and there is a heaven and hell, then the atheist loses everything for their belief after death as they will spend an eternity in hell for not accepting the truth about Jesus Christ. If you are going to be right or wrong, which person would you rather be? Most answer, "The Christian, of course." The Christian wins in both cases because he spends an eternity with God if he is right. If he is wrong, he wins for the sake of living a Christian life while alive and not knowing the difference at all after death.

To put it in worldly monetary terms, the Christian is like a billionaire who bets a dollar on a wager. What does the billionaire lose if he is wrong? A dollar. The billionaire won't notice or even be conscious of the missing dollar in the end. The atheist on the other hand is like a billionaire who bets his entire fortune on a single wager. What does this billionaire lose if he is wrong? Everything—his entire fortune. I believe true wealth is measured by love—God's love. By accepting God's love and how that love manifested into Jesus' sacrifice for us, we can spend that love in the presence of God and Christ in heaven. For the Christian, that wealth is infinite. There is no greater wealth than that. I am just not willing to gamble that much. Most would say the billionaire gambling his entire fortune on a single wager would be very irresponsible. Why then is the atheist any less irresponsible?

Having been an atheist for the first forty-two years of my life, I made all kinds of statements and proclamations about what being atheist was all about. I used to say I didn't believe in anything, I didn't put my trust in anything, and God and faith are for weak-minded people who need to lean on some false belief just to get through the day. These statements couldn't be further from the truth. I even remember the first experience I had with other children confessing my atheistic views. I was in second grade, it was a warm spring day just after recess in Ellicott City, Maryland—a historic town nestled on the Patapsco River. Each of my classmates was proclaiming their religion. "I'm Jewish," exclaimed one, and "I'm Catholic," said another. "I'm a Christian," said yet another. So on and forth, they went around the circle of kids until it came to me. I proudly announced, "I'm an atheist!" The looks of fear and query were palpable. One of the kids blurted out, "That…that is awful." I didn't understand the implications of my words at the time, only that I was just regurgitating what I heard my dad say. The other children asked, "How is that possible?" to which I answered, "Well, that is what my dad is. If it is good enough for him, it must be good for me too." I had no idea why the other kids might have thought that was strange.

As I grew older, I never really knew about or truly understood any religion. All I knew was that Christmas was Santa and presents. Easter was the Easter Bunny, painted eggs, and candy. Chanukah was some mysterious celebration my Jewish friends recognized. I had absolutely no understanding of the real meaning behind any of the holidays and why we celebrated them. On Sundays, our friends would go to church. My brother and I would patiently wait for them to return so we could all go outside and play together. As a child, I didn't feel as though I was missing anything. I thought it was okay not to believe in anything in particular.

First, to say I didn't believe in anything was false. I believed that there was no God and there was no heaven or hell or life after death. I believed in Darwin's explanation of evolution to satisfy the origins of my own existence. Those are beliefs. They aren't beliefs in a god that existed or in creation, they are beliefs that God does not exist and that we evolved from a primordial sludge.

I believed aliens existed before I believed in Jesus' death and resurrection. I believed in alien existence without a shred of evidence. There are no alien bones in the fossil record. There are no historical documents that clearly state aliens visited us here on Earth. There are no alien space crafts in any of the world's museums. There are no clear definitive photographs or videos of aliens or their space crafts. There have been individual and perhaps small groups of two or three that claim to have shaken hands with an alien or have been abducted by aliens. However, I am not aware of a mass experience where 500+ eyewitnesses testified to shaking the hand of an alien and holding a conversation all at the same sighting. Interestingly enough, though, 500+ people did see the resurrected Jesus all at the same sighting. And, there are thousands of historical documents dedicated to supporting and describing the resurrection of Jesus Christ. Was I really willing to believe in aliens but not Jesus? More importantly, was I really willing to believe in alien existence and not Jesus without ever having read the Gospels? I now see just how ridiculous that was. I am not arguing the existence of alien life at all. Even though I choose not to believe they exist, I understand—when we count up all the possible planets in the universe that life could exist on—the statistical probability of alien life existing is there.

An atheist friend of mine once challenged me with the question, "What would I do if aliens did ever come to Earth and proved their existence once and for all?" After careful thought, I said, "Nothing. The existence of aliens wouldn't change my faith in God and Christ at all."

This individual then replied, "Contact with an intelligent alien life form would cancel out the Bible and discredit Christianity completely! That event would be evidence that mankind was not the one and only focus of God."

To which I said, "I don't think it would. After all, the Bible says nothing about other intelligent species that exist here on Earth that we are fully aware of now, like dolphins and chimpanzees." I believe that is because the Bible is a story about God's relationship with and love for mankind. It is not about God's relationship with dolphins and chimps. Therefore, the Bible would make no reference to alien life on other planets because it isn't a story about God's relationship with martians. Mankind is the focus in the Bible because it represents God's love for mankind. Jesus died so that we, mankind here on earth, may live. As far as I can tell, Jesus didn't die for some other alien life form like martians.

If a martian did land on Earth and we were all introduced to him, I hope the first question we asked would be: "Does your species have a book with a similar narrative as we have in the Bible?" Knowing whether or not they had a relationship with a god that was rooted in love as well would be a good thing to know. In the meantime, I will reserve the right to change my mind about believing in the existence of aliens for when I actually meet one.

The faith I had developed as an atheist had no basis or foundation on which to build sound principles to live my life by. If I believed there was no God or life after death, then I must believe there are no consequences for my actions beyond what is written in man's law books. As a result, I believed that if you did something wrong and didn't get caught, that it was probably okay. I could cheat on this or that, I could tell a lie here and there, and as long as it was just my personal little secret, then I didn't really do anything wrong. As I look back on those years, I am horrified at just how wrong I was. I did understand the difference between right and wrong when it came to murder and other felonies. Just because a person is an atheist doesn't mean that person is a cold-blooded killer or a bank robber. It was the little things that had me confused. It was in the little things that my mind could justify and what I now understand is sin.

I remember, as a young boy, I used to love building models. At the local toy store, there was a model kit to build a World War II helicopter and it was twelve dollars. Being eight or nine years old back in the mid-1970s, twelve dollars was hard to come by. So, one day, I reached into my dad's wallet and stole twenty dollars. As if a missing twenty dollars would go unnoticed in 1976. I decided I needed to come up with a way to have come by twenty bucks so I pretended to find it out in the front yard. "It must have come blowing in the wind!" I exclaimed as I ran into the kitchen holding a crisp twenty boasting to my parents. It all sounds absurd now, but welcome to the mind of a nine-year-old atheist. As I would later find out, my parents were on to me from the beginning.

My parents did let me go to the toy store and purchase the model helicopter with my ill-gotten gains. I thought I was in the clear. I believed I had gotten away with my plan and was quite impressed with myself. I didn't feel guilt or remorse for my actions. I believed that since I had completed the caper without being discovered, what I had done was perfectly okay. Upon returning home from the store, my parents sat me down and proceeded to question me about the rather unbelievable story I concocted to explain how I found the money. Besides, my father was quite aware of his missing twenty-dollar bill. After finally coming clean and admitting to taking the money from dad's wallet, my parents explained very lovingly the reason it was wrong to steal from other people. I was then required to do extra chores around the house to repay my dad for the stolen money. In 1976, it took a lot of hours of extra chores to come up with the money I had taken. I was not able to put the model together until the debt was repaid in full. So, there the model sat on the top shelf of our toy closet for several months as a reminder not to steal.

The lesson was a good one. It included a loving explanation of right versus wrong and a lengthy punishment. I don't feel I really learned anything from it, however, other than to be more careful and perhaps come up with a better story next time; a more believable story to cover my tracks. Looking back all these years later, I realized the lesson was missing one major ingredient. It was missing a clear understanding of God's love. Without that understanding, I just didn't rationalize the nature of sin. I didn't truly understand, as a child, the difference between right and wrong when it came to the little things. I still thought that if you could just get away with any type of behavior, it was okay to behave that way.

When we understand God's love for us, we can understand the nature of sin. We can see that all sin, regardless of the degree of severity, is an act of selfishness and is in direct conflict with the selfless concept of love, God's love specifically. Therefore, all sin is bad in the eyes of God. You can't cheat just a little or lie just a little because it is all wrong and is all sin. By placing all our trust in God's full triune love, we can begin to see that the difference between right and wrong is as clear as the difference between black and white. There is no gray area. Years ago, looking at all this through the eyes of an atheist, I just saw a whole lot of gray areas.

You don't have to be just an atheist to think the gray area is an okay place to be. In fact, many Christians choose to live in the gray area as well. Christians do still sin and fall away from God. However, it is when we truly pray over God's love for us that it becomes abundantly clear that this is the wrong approach. That twinge of guilt starts to erode away at our conscience and we desire to repent. We desire to change our behavior. We can use the equation $F = TL^3$ to develop our trust in God's love and to lead us to a clearer understanding.

As an atheist, I used to think I didn't trust in anything in particular. That was false too. I did put a lot of trust in myself. I trusted that I alone was in control of my own destiny. I had nothing else to fall back on, nothing else to provide support and encouragement. It was all on me. There was no idea of heaven to trust in either. This led me to want to grab everything I could for myself. After all, I have a relatively short amount of time to make what I thought was the best of this world while I'm here. As a leader, I didn't mind stepping on a few toes to get what I wanted. I am not saying that all atheists are really mean people. You can be a kind person and an atheist. What I am saying is that it is hard not to have a selfish bent when you believe that it all just ends when you die. It is hard not to think about yourself first when the here and now is the only guarantee according to your belief. Life has a very bleak outlook from an atheist's point of view.

I also trusted in my personal possessions as a means of defining who I was and what I could accomplish. I had to have a good job, a big house in an elite neighborhood, nice cars, nice shoes…. The list went on and on. In the absence of God and God's love, I defined myself by these worldly things. I remember believing my entire identity was rooted in my career. The profession I chose supposedly had the power to define my very being. I was a financial professional and as a result, I behaved a lot like the characters in the movies portraying the Wall Street persona. That, however, was not who I was. I was a child of God. I just chose not to see that at the time. Atheism was a choice. I chose to look away from God and the Scripture and focus on the "here and now" of this world. I chose to trust in theoretical explanations to describe why the world is the way it is regardless of how much empirical evidence existed for each description.

Before the scientists get upset, I am not downplaying the advances in science and technology one iota. God has revealed to man—through science, technology, and all the sweat and tears of the brilliant individuals across all scientific disciplines—some amazing and wonderful things. As an atheist, though, I took science to be a definitive answer, the one and final truth to what the world is and all that is in it. That is just not the case as most scientists will confess. Science is a never-ending search for truth; a set of theories that remain theories until they are proven wrong. That is why they are called theories. There is the theory of evolution, the theory of electromagnetism, the theory of gravity, and so on. I liken mankind's scientific endeavors to wiping away the condensation on a foggy window. Over time, man has been able to wipe away some of the fogginess on the window, giving us just a glimpse of what lies beyond the glass. A glimpse of how the world works, of how God's creation works; but it is never a full, complete picture. It can't be as we have only been able to wipe away small patches of fog here and there from the window. The vast amount of what we don't see completely eclipses the amount of what we do see. Perhaps, in time, God will allow all of the fog to be wiped away. That will probably be very far off in the future, or perhaps it is all revealed in heaven. I certainly don't proclaim to know the answer to that. As a Christian, I have chosen to place my trust in the love of God, as through God's love, the truth will be revealed in time.

Many atheists I know lean on science in an attempt to support their atheistic views. Many believe that scientific discoveries definitively answer all our questions and even discredit the Bible. The simple fact is not one scientific discovery discredits any aspect of the Bible. The Big Bang theory and the Darwinian theory of evolution don't discredit the Book of Genesis and creation. Many theories in modern science provide a level of detail not given in the Bible. A lot of the details we find in these modern theories were left out of the Bible on purpose by God because these were details not relevant to the text. Science does, however, complement the Bible in many ways and can be thought of as an extension to many things described in the Scripture. The Book of Genesis is very vague, scientifically speaking, and leaves out most of the details. Those details are left out purposefully because they are irrelevant to the overarching story. The story of God's love for and desire to have a relationship with mankind. The "Big Bang theory" and the Book of Genesis both support the same idea that something came from nothing. Just because Genesis doesn't go into great scientific detail doesn't mean it is not the truth. The Book of Genesis doesn't describe the specific events surrounding the moment light illuminated the universe beyond **"And God said, 'Let there be light,' and there was light. And God saw that the light was good. And separated the light from the darkness" (Genesis 1:3–4 ESV)**. The Book of Genesis gives us nothing more. Nothing more is necessary at all for a story about God's love for and desired relationship with each and every human being.

I find it interesting that modern science has a similar narrative to the book of Genesis. Take String Theory for example. String theory is one of the most promising scientific theories to describe the universe. String Theory attempts to unify the four known field theories, gravitation, electromagnetism, the strong nuclear force and weak nuclear force. String theory states that all particles in the universe are not point particles but the frequency of tiny vibrating strings, Similar to how the different notes on a vibrating violin string are represented by different frequencies, each type of particle represents a different frequency of tiny vibrating strings. All that we see in the physical universe is made up of tiny vibrating strings. So how does this relate to Genesis you ask? Thousands of years ago the author of Genesis writes that creation resulted from God speaking the universe into existence. Speaking implies sound which implies a vibration that emanates the sound. The author of Genesis implies that the universe was created by a vibrating mechanism, God's voice, now, thousands of years later science's most promising description of the universe is a vibrating mechanism. Perhaps science has revealed the resonating sustain of God's voice through String Theory. After all the author of Genesis could have described God gesturing his hand or simply willing creation mentally to create the universe. The Author, however, used a vibrational description that is not far off a description fitting today's String Theory. Scientists might think this is a stretch and perhaps it is. But, if God is slowly revealing His creation to us then I think it is fitting that it has the resemblance of the original text. It is also interesting that both the book of Genesis and modern science describe a process for creation where something came from nothing. Perhaps it is just a coincidence. To think that two major aspects of creation and the very nature of the universe have similar narratives, narratives that were written thousands of years apart just lend to my inability to discredit the Bible through scientific discovery.

I have yet to read a theory of an evolutionary mechanism that explains the origin of the vast amount of information found in the genetic code of all life on earth. As a matter of fact, the theory of Darwinian evolution violates the second law of thermodynamics. The second law pertaining to entropy, as we read earlier in this book, states over time, a system will become more and more disordered. Darwin's theory of the evolution of life is a theory where more and more order is added to the system over time. This is a clear contradiction.

Who is to say the introduction of all the information in the genomes of all living things didn't require intelligent design, the intelligence of God. Life itself resembles invention and we know that invention requires intelligent design. Invention requires intelligence to put component parts together to create a more complex design that has function and purpose. Function that the component parts could not accomplish separately on their own. The human eye is a good example. Each and every component of the human eye has been designed with a very specific purpose and function. Each specified component has been combined with all the others for the purpose of capturing light then sending signals to the brain to interpret the vast amount of information that tiny photons carry when entering the eye. At this very moment, your brain is interpreting the light reflected off the page you are reading as a page in a book covered with a series of symbols (letters, punctuation, and spaces) because your eye was perfectly designed to collect the information and send it off to the brain for interpretation. There is no verifiable scientific explanation that describes how the eye came to be and where all the information that makes up an eye came from. Blind (pun intended) random processes simply don't explain it. So, it is perfectly okay to believe that an intelligent designer invented the eye because the eye resembles something invented.

Even the invention of something as simple as a pizza requires an intelligent designer, a chef, to put the component ingredients together to create the pizza. If you were to put the same component ingredients of a pizza on a counter next to an oven and gave it four billion years to become a pizza, all the combined possible blind, random processes would never produce a hot, cheesy pepperoni pizza. The blind random processes of evolutionary theory lack the ability to discredit intelligent design completely.

All the modern discoveries of the nineteenth, twentieth, and now twenty-first centuries such as electromagnetism, quantum mechanics, relativity, theoretical physics, cosmology, and medicine take nothing away from biblical truth; therefore, they aren't foundations on which to support atheism. The Bible is a love story about God's relationship with mankind. The Bible isn't a scientific thesis. The Bible leaves out all the information regarding the inner workings of the universe on purpose because it just isn't relevant to the story. Having a full understanding of quantum mechanics or genomics is not required to understand God's love or God's desire for a relationship with us. So, to look to the Bible's lack of scientific reference to all we have learned over the last two thousand years to discredit the Bible is a poor argument at best.

I often speak to atheists who have never really done any research into their own belief. I was guilty of this myself. Many have never read the Bible and many have very little understanding of the different scientific disciplines. They rely on bits of information shared as social media posts, reported on television, or published in popular magazines. That is not to say that all atheists are not educated in science and theology. It is just that I have met very few.

I recently asked a skeptic why he put no faith or trust in the Bible. He gave me a one-word response, "Science." So, I probed a little further. I asked, "To what branch or discipline of science are you referring?" He replied, "I don't know exactly. I suppose all of them." This self-proclaimed skeptic wasn't making it easy. I then asked him, "Give me an example of a specific scientific discipline that would cause you to feel it discredited the Bible." He replied again with a one-word answer, "Evolution." I sensed

I wasn't getting anywhere, so I tried one more time. I asked, "Which definition of evolution are you referring to? Evolution represents a gradual change over time; evolution refers to the idea that all living things originated from a common ancestor; or evolution refers to natural selection through random mutations where mutations that allow for a stronger, more fit life form are then passed on to the next generation through the reproductive process?" To which I got a blank stare. It was clear that this individual had no idea why he didn't trust the Bible. He certainly had no real understanding as to why he chose to be an atheist. Perhaps it was ignorance or apathy that led him to make the choices he made. In either case, it is a reckless approach to building faith.

Furthermore, God designed humans to be very inquisitive. We have a deep desire to know truth and to seek knowledge in pursuit of that truth. If God had unveiled all his secrets from the beginning and laid it all out in the form of biblical text, we would have a very boring existence. We would have little to look forward to. Discovery is exciting for almost everyone I know. Every stage of life comes with new discovery. It drives mankind forward and gives us a sense of purpose. God knows our desire to seek knowledge and has created a universe full of his secrets to discover. The desire for knowledge started in the Garden of Eden when Adam and Eve took a bite of the forbidden fruit to gain the knowledge of good and evil. Human beings have been seeking knowledge ever since. When a new scientific discovery is announced, it usually comes with great excitement. We read about it in newspapers, online, through social media, and watch it on television. How boring would our existence be if it were all given to us from the beginning of time. The desire for knowledge and the intellect to go and seek it are wonderful gifts from God. It is perfectly okay to be a seeker of knowledge such as a scientist, doctor, or mathematician and believe in God and the biblical truth. Those disciplines take nothing away from God or the Bible.

Science has a wonderful place in God's creation as a playground for the inquisitive mind of mankind. I love reading about all sorts of scientific disciplines. I don't, however, see them as a source of information that takes anything away from the Bible or the existence of God for that matter. I did as an atheist and finally came to the conclusion that science just doesn't accomplish such a feat. The Bible represents love and a relationship. I can find all the truth of the Bible intuitively as I outlined in the second chapter of this book. Atheism can't stand firmly on any field of science as a foundation for a faith in "no God" exists.

I mentioned at the beginning of this chapter that, as an atheist, I believed that God and faith are for weak-minded people who need to lean on some false belief just to get through the day. I couldn't have been more wrong. I didn't realize at the time how weak I was as an atheist. It takes far more energy and strength to keep one's eyes open then to allow them to close. As an atheist, I chose to close my eyes to God and all that he represents. That is actually very easy to do. I mentioned that I trusted in myself as an atheist. The self has a pull, a kind of gravity that drags us and our focus back in on ourselves. It doesn't require much strength at all to be selfish. We all seem to be drawn inwardly to ourselves. That is, after all, the nature of sin. We are all born with a sinful nature—selfishness. That being the case, it would require a great deal more strength to focus away from ourselves and pour into others what God has poured into us. I have found that I am much stronger as a Christian because I had to exercise strength to leave my selfish, inwardly focused ways.

There is also a collective strength I found in the Body of Christ. As I walked in community with other Christians in prayer and worship, I discovered additional strength that was shared collectively. This was a profound moment in destroying the barriers of my faith in Jesus. My atheistic beliefs began to disintegrate. Leaning on the belief that I would be weak if I believed in God crumbled under my own weight and was not foundational for the faith I had as an atheist. The equation $F = T(A_n)$ had completely failed me as a viable foundation for a faith on which to build life-giving principles.

For those of you keeping score, you may have noticed that in this whole chapter dedicated to atheism, I only made one reference to a verse from the Scripture. I did that to represent the emptiness one feels in the absence of God's Word. If you are like me and desire God's Word, then I know you were looking for it. You were craving it. I know because I was craving it. As an atheist, I lived without the Word of God applied to my everyday life. Looking back on those years, I can clearly see the emptiness I felt without his word. Placing my trust and ultimately my faith in a universe that ends in complete nothing was a sad and bleak existence. When I look out into the world around me and the universe beyond, I see a whole lot of something. To believe that it all just vanishes with death makes no sense to me at all anymore.

The equation $F = T(A_n)$ fails on all points as a foundation on which to develop a sound faith. There isn't a single argument that allows for truth in a belief that no God exists. Not even all the scientific discoveries of the last four hundred years definitely disprove the existence of God. I can't see any reason to not trust in the love of God. I praise Jesus Christ every day for allowing my eyes to be opened to a truth that can't be denied.

CHAPTER 11

AN ADDICTION

$F = T(Df_A)$: Faith equals trust in desires of the flesh and addictions. This chapter has proved to be the hardest yet most enlightening chapter to write because we all struggle with desires of the flesh, and for some, it leads to debilitating addictions. Addiction comes in all forms. When we think of addiction, most jump to thoughts of drug addicts and alcoholics, but these don't begin to scratch the surface. There is drug addiction, alcohol addiction, sexual addiction, body modification addiction, behavioral addictions, the list goes on and on.

"I can do all things through him who strengthens me."
(PHILIPPIANS 4:13 ESV)

"Therefore, if anyone is in Christ, he is a new creation. The old has passed away; behold, the new has come."
(2 CORINTHIANS 5:17 ESV)

For the purpose of this book, let's define desires of the flesh as the things that make us feel good; things that can help to mask the pain and anxiety of everyday life. These are things that bring only temporary relief to the pain we experience throughout our lives here in the world. This temporary relief is usually brought on by chemicals being released into our bodies such as endorphins. Endorphins are any of a group of hormones secreted within the brain and nervous system having a number of physiological functions. They are peptides which activate the body's opiate receptors, causing an analgesic effect. Endorphins are essentially the brain's "feel good" chemicals.

The feelings of pleasure we get from our desires of the flesh are just temporary and therefore not constant. They could never replace the constant of God's love for us as a foundational constant for our faith, yet so many people fall prey to the enemy and pursue these desires as if they could. The desires become such a focus in life that, in time, can manifest into addictions and addictive behavior. The quick fix fades as fast as it comes and requires constant feeding to keep up with it. God's love is the opposite of this—it never fades. God's love is always feeding us through the Holy Spirit. The numbing effects we experience from addictive behavior can blind us to the presence of God's love. Drug and alcohol addiction are among the most prevalent addictions in our society today and have become epidemics. Addiction does not know the color of your skin, how wealthy or poor you are, or even what language you speak. Addiction can affect anyone from any walk of life.

To place all our trust in the pursuit of the gratification of our own desires instead of God's love will result in disaster. First, desires of the flesh are the most temporary fleeting things we could choose to pursue. Satisfying our urges and desires result in a very short-lived period of good feeling. This sense of euphoria may only last a few minutes or a few hours and always leaves us seeking more. There is no fulfillment and certainly no contentment that comes with the pursuit. We are left feeling empty, needing more and more in a fleeting attempt to constantly satisfy the desire. There is absolutely nothing constant about our desires of the flesh. They fail on all levels at replacing God's love in our faith equation. It is this never-ending attempt to chase after temporary feelings of euphoria that can lead to a life of addiction. The process can be both psychological and chemical. When that happens, we find ourselves with a dependency—a dependency that can ruin lives and families altogether.

Addiction is a real thing and is not to be taken lightly. Many times, the best approach is to seek out professional help; to seek out someone whom God has placed a gift in to help those struggling with addiction and mental health issues such as psychiatrists, psychologists, addiction counselors, and the like. Seeking out professional help does not mean you should not seek out help through God and the Body of Christ, though. Church leaders and church groups are wonderful sources of support. Developing a relationship with others who may have or are still struggling with the same issues can provide additional strength to those seeking healing. Perhaps one can find inspiration through another person who had dealt with similar struggles and now has the wisdom to pour out God's love onto those still struggling. Combining professional help with the love of God poured out by the Body of Christ is very important. Focusing on God's love for us is a major factor in recovering from addiction. This can be illustrated in the equation $F = TL^3$. Let's explore this in further detail.

Many drug addicts and alcoholics whom I have spoken with over the years often tell me that they believe their addictions started out as a way to numb the trials of reality; to block out the pain, suffering, and anxiety that they have had to endure throughout life here in the world. They go on to explain that they eventually overcome the intense draw of the addiction through God's love. Learning to accept God's love and declaring their lives to Jesus Christ became a major turning point in their lives. This is a theme I hear time and time again. Addicts could only get so far on their own or with professional help. They will tell you that the counselors, treatment centers, and doctors were invaluable but would only get them so far around the track. It would be the additional strength they received through Jesus Christ that would get them across the finish line. Without God, they so often fall back into their old addictive ways.

Pastor George Wood of the Timothy Initiative in Tampa, Florida experienced this firsthand. I had the pleasure of meeting Pastor George

Wood through an initiative to bring faith leaders together to combat the opioid crisis in Hillsborough County, Florida. Pastor George heads up the Timothy Initiative which is a men's ministry to help men with drug and alcohol addiction. Pastor George is also with Tampa Underground, a group of over 200 micro churches (small missional communities) in the Tampa Bay area and beyond.

George's childhood was plagued with physical and mental abuse. George's brother and sister also experienced similar abuse. The abuse robbed these three of their childhood and feelings of self-worth. The trauma George and his siblings endured led them all to a life of drug and alcohol addiction that began during their early teens. George just wanted to forget the abuse and all the pain that resulted from it.

George said, "Addiction is like the constant gnashing of teeth tearing you down day after day, week after week, month after month, and year after year until, eventually, you are just a shell of your former self." George would regularly party and do drugs with his brother. They were a partying "dynamic duo" of sorts. The two, however, would go on to take two very different paths in life. George's brother attended Harvard Law School and became an attorney in the Tampa Bay area. George, on the other hand, partied and abused drugs and alcohol for many years until he ended up in the county jail and hit rock bottom. George realized he just couldn't go on living life by hiding from his painful past. That was the year 2005. In 2006, George started recovery from his addictions and found Jesus Christ. This was George's turning point.

After years of pain and self-destructive behavior, George came to Christ and started turning his life around. It wasn't an easy process. There was dealing with the abuse he endured throughout his childhood from the perspective of his new "sober" self. This meant reliving a lot of pain and heartache without hiding behind the drugs and alcohol. The love of Christ gave him the strength and determination to fight his addictions. George battled through his recovery all the while watching his brother and sister continue on with their addictions. George tried very hard to get his siblings to Christ and start down the road to recovery. That, however, just wasn't meant to be.

In 2009, George's sister overdosed and died. Several months later, George's brother, a prominent lawyer in Tampa, also succumbed to his addiction and overdosed as well. George's world was crashing down around him with the deaths of his two siblings. George was tempted to give up and go back to a life of drug addiction. Something, however, kept him from doing that. George will tell you that it was God's deep, steadfast love that kept him sober through the insurmountable pain of losing both of his siblings to the life of addiction he once shared with them. With God's love supporting him, George decided to devote his life to ministry. One faith-filled day, like a rising phoenix out of the ashes of two tragic deaths—the deaths of his two siblings, George birthed the "Timothy Initiative."

"But for that very reason I was shown mercy so that in me, the worst sinners, Christ Jesus might display his immense patience as an example for those who would believe in him and receive eternal life."

(1 TIMOTHY 1:16 NIV)

George told me the Timothy Initiative exists for broken men. In the face of addiction, homelessness, depression, and incarceration, the Timothy Initiative helps to restore men as they are healed through the love of Jesus Christ. It is a model that centers on community, discipleship in Christ, recovery, and work therapy. George started a construction company to employ the forty plus men in his program here in Tampa. George explained to me that he had no idea how to do construction. One day, however, the Holy Spirit just dropped the knowledge into him. George said, "I just woke up one morning knowing how to build an entire house."

As George embarked on this new journey into construction through Timothy Initiative, people would comment, "You must have been doing this for years." To which he would reply, "No, actually, just a few months."

What a wonderful representation of the power of God's love for George and the men he ministers to. The Timothy Initiative is not just about recovery, it is about community and growing as a person in Christ. The men live in community with one another, they pray together and minister to each other. There is no time limit or expiration date to someone's stay at Timothy Initiative. The process is open ended. Men can remain in the program, in the community for as long as it takes to fully heal. The program revolves around Christ's love. I see the power of the term L^3, the triune love of God, in the Timothy Initiative and in everything these men do.

Pastor George is an inspiration and example of just how God's love can empower each and every one of us regardless of our current or past circumstances. God has a plan for each of us and he expects us to move from here to there in the process. Pastor George's "there" was a place of debilitating addiction and pain. God's plan was to move him to his "here"—a place of service, love, and peace of mind. Pastor George's "here" has a purpose. He is changing lives for the better. God uses broken people and Pastor George is being used by God in profound ways. Pastor George chose to stop turning his back on God. Now he leans in toward God, arms wide open to accept all of God's love and grace so he can pour it back out into others who are hurting and struggling in his community.

To learn more about the Timothy Initiative, go to www. timothyinitiative.org.

The feeling we get from the high we receive from drug use is very temporary. When the high becomes our primary pursuit, it can lead to death. As we saw in Pastor George's story, addiction doesn't always end well. Just as the enemy took the lives of George's siblings far too early in life, my paternal grandfather, too, succumbed to the perils of alcohol addiction. My grandfather was an alcoholic. My father would tell me stories of walking down the hallway of his childhood home, passing his parents' bedroom, and being overwhelmed by the stench of booze and vomit. He would tell me that his father was an angry drunk. There were also rumors of his father sexually abusing his younger sister. My grandfather took his own life when my dad was just thirteen years old. He completely missed out on his children's lives and ended his own far too early. Addiction is a sickness that can be healed. However, it does need to be caught in time. For my grandfather and George's siblings, it was too late, but it doesn't have to be for others.

> **"Is anyone among you sick? Let them call the elders of the church to pray over them and anoint them with oil in the name of the Lord. And the prayer offered in faith will make the sick person well; the Lord will raise them up. If they have sinned, they will be forgiven."**
>
> **(JAMES 5:14-15 NIV)**

I often imagine what the outcome for my grandfather would have been had he found Christ in time. Perhaps he could have had a better relationship with his children and ultimately his grandchildren. There are eight grandkids who would have loved to know him. He was a brilliant engineer, inventor, and craftsman. He handmade furniture, tools, and toys. The toys he might have made for his grandchildren could have been wonderful heirlooms passed down to their kids and perhaps to their children. But those handmade toys don't exist. My grandfather didn't find his way to the professional help he needed and certainly didn't find his way to God. Addiction isn't just about hurting the addict, it has a ripple-down effect that can impact generations. This is why it is so important to seek help as early as possible, not just professionally but spiritually as well. We read in **James 5:14-15 NIV**, God's love has the power to heal.

As I think about addiction and the desires of the flesh, I realize that the scope is far greater than just drugs and alcohol. There is sex, food, and all the things of the material world that we discussed in Chapter 6. Sex is a big one. Sexual desires manifest themselves in many ways. Some are healthy as we see in a healthy, vibrant marriage. Many are unhealthy and can lead to behaviors that promote human trafficking such as pornography and prostitution. Sexual addiction can be just as dangerous as drug addiction.

> **"That is why a man leaves his father and mother and is united to his wife, and they become one flesh."**
>
> **(Genesis 2:24 NIV)**

Biblically, sex is viewed as a gift from God when it is kept in the confines of marriage. There are countless passages in the Bible that promote a healthy intimate relationship with one's spouse. Sex is not a bad thing. The Song of Solomon is a beautiful example of God's gift of intimacy in marriage to mankind. The Bible is, however, very clear on God's stance when it comes to sexual immorality or more precisely put—sex outside the confines of marriage. Sex in this case is a sin in God's eyes. It has become corrupted when experienced outside of a healthy, loving marriage. The euphoria experienced from sex truly only has meaning when it is combined with the intimacy and love developed between two people joined in marriage by God. It is the commitment two people make to each other that gives what is otherwise a temporary fleeting sense of euphoria, the power to cement a relationship. Outside of this, that very same euphoria diminishes as a result of not being anchored in God's purposefully and very beautifully designed construct of marriage.

> **"Marriage should be honored by all, and the marriage bed kept pure, for God will judge the adulterer and the sexually immoral."**
>
> **(Hebrews 13:4 NIV)**

I know many men and women who believed that they could be fulfilled by having multiple sexual partners. They were lying to themselves. They were living a dangerous life that could lead to the transmission of diseases like gonorrhea, chlamydia, syphilis, hepatitis, and HIV. When I would ask them about the potential diseases they could catch, they would always reply with, "I am very careful," or "I always take precautions." Many of these individuals turn away from God and Christ because they feel that they should be able to have sex any time they want. After all, no one gets hurt when two consenting adults engage in the act of sex. The truth is, someone does get hurt. God designed intimacy for the confines of a committed relationship in marriage. That being the case, we lose something deeply rooted within ourselves when we jump from one partner to another because there is an emotional piece of the puzzle that gets left behind with every partner. In time, a real pain develops and one can be left with a deep sense of emptiness and loneliness.

> **"It is God's will that you should be sanctified: that you should avoid sexual immorality; that each of you should learn to control your own body in a way that is holy and honorable…"**
>
> (1 THESSALONIANS 4:3–4 NIV)

Refraining from sex while living a single life in today's society can be very difficult. We are enticed by the enemy everywhere we look. We see sexually provocative images in magazines, on billboards, on television, and in movies. Learning to control this powerful desire is one of the hardest things for us to do. This is where placing all our trust in the love of God is critical. I love the phrase "Keep your eyes on the prize." It is important to understand that the prize is Jesus! It is not your next sexual conquest. My good friend, Jacob, puts it this way: "You need your theology to be stronger than your biology." This makes a lot of sense to me. When we place our trust in God's love and focus on the process through the equation $F = TL^3$, we can fully understand just how strong our theology can be. It is a constant battle that I struggled with my entire life as a single adult. Prior to accepting Jesus as my savior, I didn't think twice about having multiple partners a week. There was a tremendous feeling of guilt that ultimately welled up inside of me after several years of living this way. I found myself looking for more when I had no idea of what "more" even was.

"But I say to you that everyone who looks at a woman with lustful intent has already committed adultery with her in his heart."

(MATTHEW 5:28 ESV)

Even now, in a committed relationship with my spouse, I struggle daily with this fleshy desire. We live in a world where people dress provocatively. I know when I see a beautiful woman that my mind goes to a place it shouldn't be going. Most men I know would confess the same. This is when I have to consciously think about this one simple equation to help me focus back on Jesus and calm the sexual storm that inevitably starts to swell up inside me. It is through God's love that I try so hard to put my mind in the right place. God's place. To be honest, I don't always succeed. God knows that I won't always succeed. That is where the anchor—his steadfast, constant love for me—comes into play, and I am able to find my way back to God. I know I can't do it without God's love because I spent years attempting to do just that as an atheist. I failed time and time again back then.

There are many more desires that lead to addiction than I covered here in this chapter, and they are all just as dangerous and real as the ones mentioned herein. The equation $F = T(Df_A)^\wedge$ fails terribly as a sound, foundational expression for faith. Desires of the flesh are only inwardly focused. That means that they only satisfy selfish desires. They never express an outward flow of love and service to God or others. They are very temporary and leave us feeling empty and wanting for more. Desires of the flesh are corruptible. They can lead to crimes such as drug dealing, robbery, prostitution, and even murder. God's love, on the other hand, is none of this. God's love is permanent, incorruptible, and completely fills us full of all the joy we need to experience in our lives; something that drugs, sex, food, money, or career can never do.

God's love and the constant never-ending pursuit of that love can help to pull us from the devastating depths of addiction. God's love can free us from the pain and suffering we feel as an after effect of experiencing this broken and sinful world. I encourage anyone going through a season of addiction or pursuit of selfish desires to focus on and pray over the equation $F = TL^3$ as a way of putting God's love for you into perspective, and to begin the journey toward recovery through a relationship with Jesus Christ.

CHAPTER 12

JUST LOVE PART II

C hapter 1 opens with the words "just love." Two simple yet dynamic words that take on so much meaning. We see just how important love is, and more specifically, the value God's love brings to each and every one of us. The equation $F = TL^3$ is a simple illustration expressing that value. We see that the more trust we place in the steadfast, rock solid, limitless, never failing love of God, the greater the value we can assign to our faith. A faith that becomes the foundation for the principles by which we build our lives on. There is more to this equation, though. By placing greater and greater amounts of trust in God's love, we can begin to see the nature of God's love and the nature of love here on earth as his love is poured into us and through us by the Holy Spirit.

We have learned that love is the ultimate expression of truth and that love is sacrificial. We have also learned that whenever we "do" something for another, we are sacrificing the opportunity to "do" for ourselves and this creates an outward focus—a focus away from ourselves and toward others. An inward focus is selfishness as it is an act for the self. Love is completely outward focusing and represents the love God has for us. The love offered to us by the Father, Son, and Holy Spirit is the greatest gift of all. That gift of love is a piece of God himself. It represents the deepest, most intimate part of God. That is why he desires so much for us to freely receive and return the love he has given us. As humans, we know the pain of heartbreak when we give love—the deepest, most intimate part of ourselves—to another only to be rejected. It hurts! God feels the same when we reject his love. **"And the Lord regretted that he had made man on the earth, and it grieved him to his heart" (Genesis 6:6 ESV).**

The funny thing about love is love can't be forced, coerced, pressured, or compelled. You can't make someone love. You can't say to someone, "You better love me or I am going to do something really bad to you!" That is just not how it works. In this example, a person may pretend to love the intimidator out of fear of reprisal, but that would not be love. It would just be behavior that mimics love out of fear. There are people in places of power who use this tactic to try and coerce others to love them, but they don't love them—they fear them. In fact, the one thing God is incapable of doing is forcing love. The very act of forcing love negates love. It completely devalues the love, rendering it disingenuous and therefore nonexistent.

Love cannot be bought. Giving gifts and or money to someone with the hopes that it is what will cause them to love you doesn't work. Giving gifts with an expectation of getting something in return like love will fail at producing true love. The receiver of the gift will be enamored by the gifts, not the giver. In fact, the giver of gifts in this scenario will actually be supporting the sinful behavior of the person they are gifting to. The person receiving the gifts may pretend to love the giver for the gifts, not for who the giver is as a person, and that is a form of idolatry. Pursuing material gifts is just another sin because it is an act of self-gratification and even greed. The giver may actually be feeding the sinful behavior of whoever is receiving the gifts. In this situation, who is a sinner? The person attempting to coerce love by giving gifts or the receiver of the gifts who is pretending to love just to keep receiving the gifts? The answer is both. We all know people who have gotten involved in a relationship for what material possessions the relationship will yield. We call these people nasty names like "gold diggers" and "sugar daddies."

I am certainly not saying that you can't give gifts to express your love for someone. That is perfectly okay. It is when your motives are rooted in expectations—when you expect something in return for the gift—that it is wrong. Giving gifts as an expression of true love is done without expectations of getting something in return. We give freely out of love just because we love, not because we want something in return.

The Bible commands us to love God with all our heart, mind, and soul and to love each other as we love ourselves. This commandment is a request, a deep desire of God, and a choice given to mankind as an act of free will. Love can only be given freely, received freely, and returned freely. Love must come full circle to be fulfilled. God designed love to be reciprocal. God gave us his love and we must freely receive it and give it back to God to complete the cycle. If this is true, then love is an act of "free will." By working through the equation $F = TL^3$, we can unlock the very nature of "free will." Perhaps, this is why free will even exists at all. Perhaps, God designed free will specifically for love. I believe that is the purpose of free will. God could not design love without it. God so desires us to freely return his love because it is the one thing he can't force on us. God knows in his infinite wisdom that if he were to "make" us love him and make us love others, that very act would invalidate the love altogether. The love would not be genuine. If love isn't given freely, it isn't love at all and is completely disingenuous. I believe that the reciprocal nature of love is woven into the essence of the symmetry and balance God used to design the universe.

This is another example of why I believe a loving god that desires a relationship with each and every one of us represents the one true God. A god that just desires obedience from us doesn't make sense to me. If we were here just to obey a bunch of rules, why wouldn't that god just make us do so? Forcing someone to obey a rule or law doesn't invalidate the rule or law. Nothing is lost in the value of the rule or law when one is forced, made, or coerced to follow and adhere to those laws and rules. Love, however, loses all its value when it is forced. Therefore, it is not love at all.

Jesus even asks us to freely love our enemies, to turn the other cheek and forgive. Each and every time we choose to love, it is an act of free will. God has freely given us his love through his grace. **"For it is by grace you have been saved, through faith—and this is not from yourselves, it is the gift of God…"** (Ephesians 2:8 NIV). God desires us to freely receive that love and to freely return it to him. **"And so we know and rely on the love God has for us. God is love. Whoever lives in love lives in God, and God in them"** (1 John 4:16 NIV).

Love does not exist in the absence of free will. Free will is the heart-beat that allows love to freely flow from God to us and from us to God, from one person to another and back again. Sure, we have the ability to make choices about other things in our lives and free will seems to have spilled over into other aspects of decision-making, but it was originally designed for the most valuable commodity in the universe—love, God's Love. It was when Adam and Eve in the garden chose to reject God's love and sin against him for their own personal gain—to be like God and have the knowledge of good and evil that man exercised free will. This was the first act of free will that led to mankind's fall in the garden. Mankind chose in that moment to turn away from God's love.

Sin is rooted in selfishness. I can't think of a single sin that isn't born from selfishness. Idolatry is also rooted in selfishness. Every idol-atrous term used to replace God's love in the previous chapters are all for personal gain, self-satisfaction, and self-gratification. Love is a two-way street. Love must be returned freely. Worldly things are incapable of returning love and only satisfy selfish desires.

"Let no one say when he is tempted, 'I am being tempted by God,' for God cannot be tempted with evil, and he himself tempts no one. But each person is tempted when he is lured and enticed by his own desire."

(JAMES 1:13–14 ESV)

Since material, worldly things are incapable of returning love, let alone returning it freely, choosing to love such things before God is sinful. Money can't love you back, power can't love you back, and as a result, can't complete the circle of love. If God designed love to be reciprocal and we choose to trust in, pursue, and love worldly things that are incapable of reciprocating the love we give, then it is easy to understand why placing those things before God would be considered sinful. This is the proverbial *"slap"* in God's face. We see this here on earth, in our relationship with others as well. We have heard stories where a husband loves his car or some other object so much that his wife feels rejected and seeks out to destroy the object of her husband's affection. In the Hollywood depictions of these stories, the wife usually destroys the car in grand fashion by blowing it up or sending it crashing off a cliff, sometimes with herself in it. These are the stories of real pain and heartache; pain many of us here on earth have felt. Why do we think it would be any less painful for God?

"May our Lord Jesus Christ himself and God our Father, who loved us and by his grace gave us eternal encouragement and good hope..."

(2 Thessalonians 2:16 NIV)

Working through the equation $F = TL^3$ has given us insight into the very nature of free will. It has unlocked our understanding that God's sacrificial love represents pure truth. If by placing our full trust in the triune love of God strengthens our faith and allows us to see the truth of the Gospel, then the two words that opened this book, "just love," take on more meaning than we could ever imagine. God designed all of mankind to simply "just love." This is the true meaning of life itself.

God has a purpose for everything he creates, including us. **"For this is what the Lord says—he who created the heavens, he is God; he who fashioned and made the earth, he founded it; he did not create it to be empty, but formed it to be inhabited..." (Isaiah 45:18 NIV).**

The Bible tells us that God's greatest commandment is to love God with all your heart, mind, and soul, and the second is to love our neighbor as we would ourselves. Man has been asking age-old questions such as, "What is the meaning of life? Why does mankind even exist?" The answer has been right in front of us for over two thousand years as the written word of God in the Bible; in the Books of Leviticus, Deuteronomy, and the Gospel of Matthew to be precise.

> **"You shall not take vengeance or bear a grudge against the sons of your own people, but you shall love your neighbor as yourself: I am the Lord."**
>
> **(LEVITICUS 19:18 ESV)**

> **"You shall love the Lord your God with all your heart and with all your soul and with all your might. And these words that I command you today shall be on your heart."**
>
> **(DEUTERONOMY 6:5–6 ESV)**

> **"Jesus replied: 'Love the Lord your God with all your heart and with all your soul and with all your mind.' This is the first and greatest commandment. And the second is like it: 'Love your neighbor as yourself. All the Law and the Prophets hang on these two commandments."**
>
> **(MATTHEW 22:37–40 NIV)**

The Bible tells us that God is love. We know intuitively that the Bible is true and represents truth, so we can trust the Bible and its implications of our very existence. **First Book of John** gives us a very clear understanding that mankind exists to love. **"Beloved, let us love one another, for love is from God, and whoever loves has been born of God and knows God. Anyone who does not love does not know God, because <u>God is love</u>. In this the love of God was made manifest among us, that**

God sent his only Son into the world, so that we might live through him" (1 John 4:7–9 ESV, emphasis mine).

Colossians 3:14 also speaks to the meaning of life being "to love." **"And above all these put on love, which binds everything together in perfect harmony. And let the peace of Christ rule in your hearts, to which indeed you were called in one body. And be thankful"** (Colossians 3:14–15 ESV).

God made each of us in his image and deeply desires us to love. We know this to be true because love has to be true. Love can't be false. This all points to one beautiful conclusion—that the meaning of life, the reason mankind exists, is to *just love*. There is no other conclusion to come to. By working our way through the equation $F = TL^3$, placing *all* our trust in the triune love of God, we can begin to see why we are here, why the universe and everything in it is here. It is all a product of God's infinite, steadfast, never failing love. It points to Jesus as well because Jesus' time on earth was the ultimate expression of God's sacrificial love for all mankind. Jesus gave his life for our salvation. The enormity of that love is breathtakingly beautiful. I can think of no greater place to put my complete trust. "God, I love you for loving me!"

CHAPTER 13

THE SOLUTION

To summarize the major points that the equation $F = TL^3$ has uncovered for us throughout this book, let's revisit those points. First, math is a universal language. The concept of 1+1=2 is the same for all people regardless of race, religion, ethnicity, nationality, or language. Even a person living in the middle of a jungle with no formal education knows that if they pick up one coconut from the jungle floor then pick up another coconut, they now have two coconuts. Regardless of the word they use for the number two, whether it be *dos*, *mbili*, or *zwei*, 1+1=2 is universally understood.

Second, mathematics is the language of God himself. Everything we see in the visible universe can be expressed mathematically. Light being emitted from the sun and distant stars can be expressed mathematically; the molecular structure of compounds can be expressed mathematically; how the planets, stars, and galaxies swirl through the cosmos can be expressed mathematically; the human genome can be expressed mathematically. Genesis tells us that God spoke creation. Every act of creation in the Book of Genesis begins with "And God said." God used language to speak the universe and everything in it into existence. He used the language of mathematics. God spoke the very fabric of the universe into existence by weaving it together with threads spun from the wool of all the mathematical disciplines.

Now, since faith plays such a vital role in the development of the principles we live our lives by, it is very important to make sure that what we are placing our trust in is, in fact, true and is the ultimate truth. How do we know God's love is the ultimate truth? The answer is right in front of us. Love is the ultimate expression of truth. We all know this to be true. You don't need a PhD to understand this. We all know this intuitively. When we think of our own love such as the love of our children, we know it to be true. When we ask ourselves how true is our love for our children, spouse, family, and friends, nothing could be truer. No one has ever said, "I love my children, but that is not really true." We truly love the people we love. That is why we call it "true love." Because love is true, love is truth, and false love can't exist because false love isn't love at all. False love is something else other than love altogether.

Since we know love is true, we also understand that true love is sacrificial. As parents, we sacrifice for the love of our children. As husbands and wives, we sacrifice so much for our spouse. Sacrificing for someone else, whether it be a big sacrifice or a small one, is when we put love into action. Something as small as reading a book to a child is sacrifice. The reader has sacrificed the time to do something for himself and spent it reading to a child. Many people would even lay down their lives for their children or spouse. That would be considered a very big sacrifice, the greatest of all sacrifices. God's love is true love because he did just that. God made the greatest sacrifice for all mankind. He came to earth in the form of his only Son and he died on the cross so we all may live. It *all* hinges on God's love for us. It all hinges on Jesus. Without God's love, perhaps creation never happens. Without God's love, mankind would never be pursued and Jesus would never have come to save us. It is all a product of God's love for you and me.

The written word of God, the Bible, is the authority by which we know that God loves us. The Bible is all about God's love for us. The Bible is rooted in love and therefore rooted in truth since love is the ultimate expression of truth. One of the unique features of this biblical love story is the object of God's love in the Bible is you and me—the readers. We are the object of the love being expressed. In most love stories, the object of a character's love is another character in the story. Earlier in this book, I used the example of William Shakespeare's *Romeo and Juliet*. In this story, the object of Romeo's love is Juliet and the object of Juliet's love is Romeo. The fact that the reader is the object of the love being expressed is unique and beautiful.

Another aspect of the Bible that lends to its truth is that the Bible is just too brutally honest and transparent to be false. The Bible reveals lying, cheating, stealing, lust, adultery, murder, violence, and repeated failure. If early Christians wanted to contrive a wild story just to get people to follow them, don't you think they would have painted a prettier picture? A picture that would be easier to accept? It is just not in our nature to be so honest and transparent unless we really meant to confess the truth. Read the social media posts of you and your connections to realize we typically only show our success and victories. You see posts and chats about the wonderful vacation, the promotion at work, birthdays, anniversaries, date night out at a nice restaurant, etc. We don't typically air our dirty laundry and show all our shortcomings. The stories in the Bible only make sense if, in fact, they are true. These are not stories that would have been included in the Bible if they were false. They would make no sense if they were not true. People would not have followed a path in many cases that led to their physical torture and death if it didn't represent truth. They certainly would not have if they knew it to be false.

Next, we discover—as we work out our faith through the equation $F = TL^3$—that replacing L^3 (God's full triune love) with idolatrous terms such as $\$^6$ (money), S^3 (self), A_n (atheism), and P_L (power) fail as an expression for faith that results in a foundation on which to build principles. These are just temporary, finite, corruptible terms that are incapable of receiving and returning the love we try to apply to them. This is because love is the essence of God and requires free will to exist. Love can't be forced or bought. All worldly, material things can be bought. However, love has to be given freely by choice and returned freely by another's choice. This shows us that love is reciprocal and that God expects love to be poured into someone who can freely accept and freely return the love. Worldly, material things are incapable of receiving, accepting, and returning love and certainly can't do that freely. All the idolatrous terms one could come up with to try to replace God's love with are temporary, corruptible, finite terms that are merely the products of this world. They don't follow us into heaven, but God's love does. God's love is the only steadfast, permanent, incorruptible, infinite term that actually transcends life and death. When we die, God's love is the one thing we actually take with us into heaven.

I hear the argument quite often from those struggling with the concept of God such as atheists, agnostics, or even those just a little skeptical and it goes as follows: "I don't believe in God because I don't know how a loving god could exist and allow bad things to happen to good people." This has been one of the hardest questions to answer as Christians because it is hard to really know God's reasoning. As I have prayed over and meditated on the equation $F = TL^3$, I believe I have gained at least a little insight to this very difficult question. First, let's be clear, God does not perpetrate evil onto good or bad people, that is Satan's job. So, to answer this question we first need to look at why God would create a universe where bad things *can* happen to good people. Why does Satan have the ability to guide us and perpetrate evil?

Next, we will have to ask: "If this is a God-created universe where evil *can* impact good, why would God then actually allow bad things to happen to good people?" I believe that God designed the universe to have a symmetric duality for the sole purpose of including love in his grand design. I define symmetric duality as "two equal yet opposite components of a system to allow for balance in that system." This explains why there is big and small, hot and cold, day and night, good and evil, love and hate, fear and courage, light and dark, etc. Even Newton's third law of motion states the case for this idea of symmetric duality: *"For every action there is an equal and opposite reaction."* Whether God designed the duality of the universe purposefully or he was guided by some godly law of grand design, the universe has a beautiful symmetry to it; a duality that cannot be broken. That means, unfortunately for us, if **good** things can happen to **good** people, then so can **bad** things happen to **good** people. Conversely, if bad things can happen to bad people, then good things must also happen to bad people. It seems we can't escape God's grand design for the symmetric duality of the universe. It appears to me that God had to design a universe where bad things can happen to good people to maintain a grand design of symmetric duality for the universe.

Perhaps it is this very symmetry that acts as the glue that holds God's creation, the universe, together. Just maybe, if God were to break any link in the chain of universal symmetry at any point, the whole universe would come crashing down. Perhaps Satan's dominion is a requirement. Perhaps an asymmetric universe couldn't accommodate love and free will. If love is an act of free will and we can choose to place all our trust in God's love by freely receiving it and freely returning it, then we must also be able to choose not to. If designing a universe that includes love requires a symmetric duality for love to exist, then perhaps that is the solution to the question, "How could a loving god exist and allow bad things to happen to good people?" Maybe God had to allow for the symmetric order of the universe in order to include love. God had to give this world over to Satan in order to accommodate love and free will. This is just a theory. I, of course, don't know the true answer. It does help me to understand that God's design is much greater than me and I may not be meant to know the answers to such questions. I do know that the argument above is just not enough for me to turn my back on God's love. It certainly isn't a strong enough argument to keep me rooted in my former atheist beliefs.

As I place complete trust in God's love, it becomes clear to me that God designed a symmetric duality to govern the universe and that symmetry allows for both good and evil to exist. But why? Is it just that God designed the duality of the universe purposefully, or was he guided by some godly law of grand design, or is it something else? I believe it has to do with designing a universe that can accommodate love. The one thing God can't do is force love on people. God knows that love has to be given freely to be true love. So if he were to make us already loving him without giving us the choice, then God knows it wouldn't really be love. It wouldn't really be what is the most personal and intimate aspect of God himself. The very nature of love requires free will. Love requires a choice to give or not to give, to accept or reject, and to return or not to return. We have the ability to choose one of the two states of love—to love or not to love. Love gives us a glimpse into the symmetric duality woven into the very fabric of the universe. Everything in the universe requires balance. Every action has an equal and opposite reaction. There is good and evil, war and peace, love and hate, fear and courage, and the choice to love or not to love. Through this one simple equation, we are able to understand that a loving god created a universe where *bad* things can happen to good people because *good* things can also happen to good people, and it is simply to accommodate love.

If I believe I am a good person—and I do, as most of us probably do—then should I assume only good thing must happen to me? This, fortunately or unfortunately, is just not the case. If we are in a season where a predominance of good things are happening to us, or we are in a season where a predominance of bad things are happening to us, then this represents equal and opposite aspects to the state of our existence at any point in our lives. Both states balance each other out. Both states are required in order for God to design a universe with love in it. He had to design a universe with symmetry, duality, and balance to accommodate free will and, ultimately, love. We live in a universe that was designed for the sole purpose to accommodate love.

It is through the equation $F = TL^3$ that we clearly see the universe itself was designed for love. When we fully trust in and accept God's love, the symmetric duality that gives rise to good and evil, a balance that is a product of God's love, becomes crystal clear. Love can't exist without free will. Free will requires a choice. A choice requires a yes or a no, a positive or negative response, two outcomes with equal and opposite repercussions. That is why the universe has been designed with breathtaking symmetrical duality; it is all in the name of love. There is symmetry every-where we look in the universe and it manifests itself in beauty. Amazingly, there is nothing more beautiful than love. As a matter of fact, the human brain attributes beauty to symmetry and balance.

The idea of symmetric duality explains—since humans can truly make a decision to obey God or not—the things that God wills for us, such as "to love," fail to take place at times; and the things God doesn't will for us, such as pain and suffering, do take place at times. Just as we would never will bad things to happen to our children, God never wills bad things to happen to us. As a result, we can understand why God cre-ated a universe where bad things do happen to good people. God had to design it that way in order to design a universe full of love. Of course, we would all like a universe to exist where the innocent can't be harmed, only good things happen to good people, and bad things can only happen to evil people. We should, however, be careful of what we ask for as this may result in a universe without love for the reasons described above. I am not willing to give up love. Are you?

All this helps us to understand why bad things can happen to good people; now, let's look at why God allows it. To come to the conclusion that bad events and circumstances are just bad and have no value for good is flawed human thinking. This is us leaning on our own under-standing, which the Bible warns against. If we are to place all our trust in the complete triune love of God, then we should also trust in God's understanding, his will for us and our circumstances. God, in his infinite wisdom and knowledge, sees the good that can come from what we might consider bad things or bad circumstances that we as humans endure and can't see ourselves. God, perhaps, allows us to endure such mal intended things because the final outcome results in something much better. We may not always see or understand the outcome. It may take years or even generations for the good to come to fruition. Sometimes, however, we do see the good results of enduring a season of suffering. It is easy to see when we become a better person or we see material improvement in our lives on the back end of a difficult season through God's grace.

God knows that the pain and/or suffering will lead to a greater outcome at some point in the future. God even feels our pain, but with a greater understanding of its purpose. Even physical death means something different to God. With the death of our physical bodies comes our eternal presence with God in heaven. God knows we will spend eternity with him in heaven when our physical body dies, so then, why would God consider that to be bad? He wouldn't.

I liken this idea to a parent who has a child who has been diagnosed with a life-threatening disease, such as cancer. There are treatments that are very painful, treatments that have horrible side effects that cause tremendous suffering. There are treatments that even result in the loss of limbs, like amputation. As parents, we allow our child to endure the pain and suffering of treatments like chemotherapy, bone marrow transplants, and even amputations because we have the ability to see that these treatments can cure the child and hopefully allow the child to have a long, healthy life, even if the child can't see past his or her own suffering. The child leans on his or her understanding of the suffering he or she experiences and expresses it through tears and emotions just like we do in times of our own suffering. Like God, we also feel the pain of our children, but with a greater understanding of its purpose. We are only human, and sometimes we as parents will even allow such treatments to be performed when we are not even sure that they will work. Sometimes it is a guessing game for parents and the doctors administering the treatments because we are merely human. God, however, is always certain of the outcome. God never guesses. And as a loving Father, God is always by our side when we are going through challenges and difficulties.

As humans, we often lean on our own understanding of good and evil and fail to trust in God. What seems bad to us may actually result in an amazing and glorious outcome. By trusting in God's love, we can step away from our own understanding and put our fears and anxieties on God for safekeeping. We may not see the good that results from bad experiences for some time. It may take days, weeks, or even years to truly understand God's plan for us and the good that can result from what we as humans believe to be bad. This is why God actually allows for it. Only God can see the whole picture at once. Only God can see the past, present, and future simultaneously, so God can be the only one to know what good can blossom from what we might consider being bad. As the equation $F = TL^3$ illustrates, by placing all our trust in God's love, we are able to trust God's understanding of good and evil. We are able to trust that what seems bad now will result in something greater, something better in the future.

The argument that a loving god can't exist because bad things happen to good people is a crutch we use to lean on our own understanding. Take the story of Stephen in the book of Acts. Stephen is primarily known for his death. He died as the first Christian Martyr. Stephen is stoned to death for proclaiming Jesus Christ. Stephen's death would be considered a bad thing that happened to a good God fearing man. Yet two thousand years later his name carries on in the Bible as someone who would not reject Jesus as an example for all Christians to follow. God had a plan for Stephen and we are experiencing the outcome of his death to this very day arguably for good. In the crowd watching the execution is Saul. Saul was a violent persecutor of Christians. He did very bad things which can be argued lead to his developing into one of the greatest disciples of Christ of all time after meeting the resurrected Jesus on the road to Demascus and changing his name to Paul. After being tortured, imprisoned, shipwrecked and bitten by poisonous snakes, Paul wrote close to two thirds of the New Testament. God knows ahead of time how bad things will lead to amazingly positive outcomes, we just need to trust in God.

The most obvious example in all of human history of a bad thing happening to a good person is the brutal death of Jesus Christ. Jesus was sinless and innocent of the crimes he was charged with. He professed love and forgiveness everywhere he went and championed the broken hurting people. No one is less deserving of the brutal torture and crucafixion that Jesus experienced. God knew what the outcome would be though. He knew it would lead to the salvation of millions of people over thousands of years. The disciples didn't know that at the time. They thought that it was all over. They believed for three days that it was all for nothing. Prior to the resurrection of Jesus the disciples were scattered and lost. God's plan, however, was revealed to them through the resurrection and they went on to do amazing things and turn the world upside down for the better. God has revealed to all Christians the wonderful outcome of Jesus' sacrifice. It is through us that we continue to share this good news and bring even more people to Christ. That is the beautiful result of a terrible act of violence. An act of violence that had been planned from the very beginning of creation to result in a love so beautiful that tens of thousands, perhaps hundreds of thousands would risk life and limb to share and millions more would accept as truth.

Is a parent not a loving parent because he or she would allow their child to endure the suffering effects of a life-giving treatment? I believe that would make a parent the opposite. I believe that proves a parent is a loving parent. Whether we see or understand the short-term or long-term outcome of suffering or not, making a judgment that God doesn't exist or isn't loving because bad things happen to good people is clearly not justified.

Even though we in the twenty first century have over two thousand years of God's revealing and understanding of His plan for Jesus and others throughout the Bible and the beautiful outcome that resulted from such horrific events, we as humans will, however, agonize over our pain and suffering. When things aren't going our way we will brood over the situation. We are weak and broken. We will revert to relying on our own understanding of our circumstances. My hope for you the reader is by using the equation $F = TL^{\wedge 3}$ as a simple reminder of God's great love for you and that God "has this" will help you rely on God's understanding for your life. That your anxieties and fear will melt away allowing you to experience the fullness of God's love and the peace and joy that comes from that love.

Finally, we know God is love, as we read in 1 John 4:8 and 4:16, and the universe is designed with love as the foundation for that universe. We also know that God's deepest desire, his supreme commandment, is to love him with all your heart, soul, and mind; and the second is to love others as we would ourselves. From this, we can conclude that we exist to "just love." The meaning of life is to *love*. We exist to reflect the most intimate part of God—his love, outwardly onto and into others. We exist to abandon selfishly inward acts of sin and just love. We no longer have to ask the questions "Why do we exist?" or "What is the meaning of life?" We know biblically that the answer to such questions is simply "To love."

> **"I have said these things to you, that in me you may have peace. In the world you will have tribulation. But take heart; I have overcome the world."**
>
> **(JOHN 16:33 ESV)**

Love comes with a very high price. A price that Jesus was willing to pay on the cross. A price that many have paid here on earth. God tells us in the Bible that it won't be easy; there will be struggles, heartache, and pain. God is telling us this because it was woven into the design of his created universe with a purpose. That purpose is love, God's love, so we may freely choose to accept it and freely choose to return it, fulfilling the reciprocal cycle that God designed love to be in the universe. If God is love, then why would he ever cheapen it? Why would it not be so valuable? It wouldn't. Because God is love, it is the most valuable thing in the universe and therefore comes with the high price that it has. The price humanity couldn't pay because we were not capable of paying it. Our broken, sinful nature left us too poor to pay it off. Jesus had to come to earth and pay the debt himself out of love for each and every one of us. The equation $F = TL^3$ has allowed me to see just how much God loves and what the true price of that love is. It was made clear by applying all of my trust in his love, strengthening my faith to such a point where it all made sense.

All the years I spent as an atheist can be summed up as being a long race to attain the prize of worldly idols, such as money, material possessions, sex, and power. These things manifest themselves in my mind as a gift-wrapped box that I can see some distance in front of me. As I fight and claw my way down the race path, I get closer and closer to the box until it is right in front of me. With all the giddiness and excitement of a child on Christmas morning, I start tearing away the wrapping paper to open my hard-earned gift. I open the box and look in only to find that it is empty. With great disappointment, I look up only to see a bigger box off in the distance. So, I continue the race, fighting and clawing my way further down this endless pursuit of worldly things. As I approach the next box, I—again with great excitement—tear away at the wrapping paper only to find another empty box. The cycle just keeps repeating. I find myself as empty as all the boxes I keep scratching and clawing to attain. This was an existence of anxiety, worry, and doubt that just left me unfulfilled and lonely.

As a Christian, I find myself surrounded by boxes filled with God's love for me and all the provision that comes with it. I am not racing down an endless path that keeps proving to produce an endless supply of empty boxes. I find myself full of joy and purpose. I have not been cured of my broken, sinful ways and have to reaffirm my faith by praying over this one simple equation each and every day. I have to take time to read God's Word and remind myself of the price of God's love every day. The enemy still attacks me. I still struggle with my fears and anxiety. However, I make it much easier on myself when I am reminding myself daily to place all my trust in God's steadfast, unfailing love. God's love and his greatest sacrifice, Jesus Christ, help me to wash away my worries, anxiety, and doubt. This one simple equation helps to illustrate just how clear it all is.

This one simple equation helps to simplify our understanding of God and Christ. As we apply all our trust in the love of God, we are also applying all our trust in God because we read in 1 John that God is love. We also know that Jesus represents the most intimate and profound love of God for us because Jesus represents God's sacrificial love. The equation $F = TL^3$ is all about God's love as is everything we see in His creation. Therefore, since God is love, the equation is also all about God; and because Jesus is the ultimate sacrifice, it is all about Jesus as well.

Illustrating the true value of God's love through the equation $F = TL^3$

gives us an easy to understand example to use when reinforcing our faith each and every day and when starting a conversation with those around us in order to spread the good news of Jesus Christ. It is my sincerest hope that the points illustrated in this God-inspired equation will help you to renew your relationship with God. That it will help you start simple conversations about God's love and biblical truth, helping each of you become better disciples. If, however, you are still skeptical, I encourage opposing arguments. Please email me your point of view at fequalstl3@gmail.com. I would love the opportunity to hear your side, think it through, and engage in a professional discussion about faith and God with you.

If this book has inspired you to accept Jesus Christ as your savior and it is the first time you have made this dedication, please join me in prayer. If you are renewing your faith once again and are looking to strengthen your relationship with Christ, please join me in prayer.

*"Father, please give me the strength and wisdom to place **all** my trust in your never-ending steadfast love because you loved me so much; your sacrificial love poured out in the death and resurrection of Jesus Christ—your Son—flows over me through the Holy Spirit. That I receive your love freely and return your love freely and accept Jesus Christ as my Lord and savior. That I live by the example of Jesus Christ and love others freely and without expectation. Allow me to renew my faith in you daily. Jesus, I am all in with you. Amen."*

This is a simple prayer that has helped me work through the equation $F = TL^3$ each and every day, strengthening my faith and my relationship with God the Father, Jesus Christ the Son, and the Holy Spirit.

It is my sincere hope that each reader of this book uses this one simple equation to spread God's love by being the best example one can be and pour love, kindness, and compassion onto everyone you encounter each and every day. It won't be easy. It will take time to get it right just some of the time. You will falter on your journey and that is okay, you are, after all, only human. I falter each day myself, but I keep striving to be the best example of Christ I can be. I am not sure if I will ever come close, but that won't stop my pursuit of Jesus and the triune love of God. To the critics, your words may sting, but I would like to think that your opposing views will allow me to think through points I have not yet considered, and perhaps help to develop better, stronger future editions of this book. In conclusion, I would like to thank each reader for taking the time to allow me to share with you the ideas illustrated by this one simple equation, and I would like you to know that I love you.

For those of you who are still wondering what the solution to the equation $F = TL^{\wedge 3}$ is, the solution is simple. You don't have to have a degree in mathematics to solve this one simple equation. The solution is simply Jesus.

CPSIA information can be obtained
at www.ICGtesting.com
Printed in the USA
LVHW021444260220
648273LV00002B/4